CAMBRIDGE TEXTS IN THE
HISTORY OF PHILOSOPHY

—

VOLTAIRE
Treatise on Tolerance

CAMBRIDGE TEXTS IN THE
HISTORY OF PHILOSOPHY

Series editors
KARL AMERIKS
Professor of Philosophy at the University of Notre Dame
DESMOND M. CLARKE
Professor of Philosophy at University College Cork

The main objective of Cambridge Texts in the History of Philosophy is to expand the range, variety and quality of texts in the history of philosophy which are available in English. The series includes texts by familiar names (such as Descartes and Kant) and also by less well-known authors. Wherever possible, texts are published in complete and unabridged form, and translations are specially commissioned for the series. Each volume contains a critical introduction together with a guide to further reading and any necessary glossaries and textual apparatus. The volumes are designed for student use at undergraduate and post-graduate level and will be of interest not only to students of philosophy, but also to a wider audience of readers in the history of science, the history of theology and the history of ideas.

For a list of titles published in the series, please see end of book.

VOLTAIRE

Treatise on Tolerance

TRANSLATED BY

BRIAN MASTERS

The Story of Elisabeth Canning and the Calas Family
An Address to the Public concerning the Parricides imputed
to the Calas and Sirven Families
An Account of the Death of the Chevalier de La Barre
The Cry of Innocent Blood

TRANSLATED AND EDITED BY

SIMON HARVEY
Queen Mary and Westfield College,
University of London

CAMBRIDGE
UNIVERSITY PRESS

PUBLISHED BY THE PRESS SYNDICATE OF THE UNIVERSITY OF CAMBRIDGE
The Pitt Building, Trumpington Street, Cambridge, United Kingdom

CAMBRIDGE UNIVERSITY PRESS
The Edinburgh Building, Cambridge CB2 2RU, UK   www.cup.cam.ac.uk
40 West 20th Street, New York, NY 10011–4211, USA   www.cup.org
10 Stamford Road, Oakleigh, Melbourne 3166, Australia
Ruiz de Alarcón 13, 28014 Madrid, Spain

First published 2000

Typeset in Ehrhardt 10/12 pt [VN]

A catalogue record for this book is available from the British Library

ISBN 0 521 64017 2 hardback
ISBN 0 521 64969 2 paperback

Transferred to digital printing 2004

Contents

Introduction

It might well be thought that Voltaire needs little introduction. He has been the subject of an enormous output of research over the years. If there is a single eighteenth-century thinker the public is generally aware of, then it is surely Voltaire. Indeed one could say that he has come to epitomise the Enlightenment in Europe. But for that very reason his work has tended to be taken for granted, even overlooked by a majority of modern readers: a giant in his own day, he has come to be regarded as *le dernier des philosophes heureux*, in Roland Barthes's memorable phrase, an outdated representative of the Age of Optimism.

Voltaire's life can be divided into several distinct periods. The formative one culminated in his visit to England in the late 1720s and in the publication of the *Lettres philosophiques* [Letters on England] in 1734. One should also mention his *Traité de métaphysique* [Treatise on metaphysics], which, while not intended for publication, was composed in 1734 and was very much influenced by English thinking. The second period of his life was marked by a long stay in the chateau of his friend Madame du Châtelet at Cirey. To this period belong the *Eléments de la philosophie de Newton* [Elements of Newton's philosophy] (the English influence is still important) and the first of his contes, *Micromégas*. Both of these works reflect Voltaire's strong interest in science at this juncture. In the mid 1740s he came out of his retreat of Cirey, but this period, although one of greater public engagement, was also a period of gradual disillusionment ('*la crise pessimiste*', as critics are fond of calling it). He experienced disappointment, first at the French court of Versailles, then at the court of Frederick the Great in Berlin, and finally in Geneva, where he received the news of the Lisbon earthquake disaster. He had also been much affected by the death of Madame du Châtelet in 1749. To this period of his life belong many of Voltaire's best-known contes: *Babouc* (1746), *Zadig* (1747), *Memnon* (1752) and ultimately the most celebrated of them all, *Candide* (1759). There was a fourth and final period to

Voltaire's life, of greatest concern to us in the volume, when he had settled at Ferney outside Geneva. The works which are associated with these highly productive years include not only the *Treatise on Tolerance* itself, but also the *Philosophical Dictionary*, the *Philosophe ignorant* [The ignorant philosopher] and *L'Ingénu* [The ingenuous one], all of which deal to some extent with the theme of intolerance.

By this stage of his life Voltaire had become one of the most famous men in Europe, his greatness acknowledged by admirers and enemies alike. But it was not only his writings and his reputation that the eighteenth-century public was acquainted with: the actual figure of him was equally familiar. It was the figure of an oldish man, rather small and gaunt, holding himself very erect with a walking stick in one hand. And the face was extraordinary too, with its hollow cheeks and mocking, cynical grin. This picture was reproduced in countless contemporary prints and circulated throughout Europe: this was 'the wise man of Ferney', as he was called. Together with this went a certain image of Voltaire, the image of a defender of the innocent. Although it was a flattering image that he took some care to promote, it was partly founded on truth. In the 1760s Voltaire had taken up many causes, the most renowned being his defence of the Protestant families of Calas and Sirven, accused of crimes they almost certainly had not committed. In the case of Calas, Voltaire arrived on the scene too late to save his life, although his innocence was subsequently established. Sirven was declared to be innocent as a direct result of Voltaire's campaign.

These activities, and others of an equally philanthropic nature (such as his efforts on behalf of La Barre and d'Etallonde), took place in the years spent at Ferney. On the Franco-Swiss border, it was, strategically speaking, a brilliant choice of residence: firstly because Voltaire could literally hop across the frontier if ever the French authorities came after him – which was a real possibility as censorship grew tighter towards the end of the Ancien Régime in France – and secondly because Ferney was no out-of-the-way retreat but a point directly on the main route between Paris and Geneva. Once he had established himself there, he turned it into a sort of clearing-house for the politically subversive ideas of the age. In fact he was so successful in making Ferney a kind of European intellectual centre that at times he became heartily sick of it and occasionally complained of being 'the innkeeper of Europe'. Ferney was hardly ever empty: a stream of distinguished visitors passed through and paid their respects to the master of the house. In this way Voltaire was able to keep in touch with all the major developments of the times. The unique importance of Ferney was that it allowed Voltaire to keep his finger on the pulse of European civilisation at a particularly crucial stage in its history.

Voltaire as philosophe

The traffic in ideas was very much a two-way affair. While books and visitors poured in, Ferney itself was a hive of activity. Voltaire had a prodigious appetite for work and he sent out a very great quantity of his own writing. Even at the age of seventy, he kept to a strict routine of ten hours of work each day, so that a vast number of pamphlets, letters and other works issued forth from Ferney for almost twenty years. In this respect Ferney gives us a clue to Voltaire's particular genius. Throughout his life he sought to absorb as many of the ideas of his age as he could, and then to make himself their vehicle. Every possible form of expression was used for the purpose: the poem, the play, the short story, the epigram, the dialogue – all form part of Voltaire's repertoire. For this reason he came to be regarded as the outstanding literary figure of the period. In fact he was merely using every resource at his disposal to carry out the job of the philosopher as he saw it, namely that of dissemination. As in the case of many other so-called philosophes in eighteenth-century France, philosophy has a special meaning for him. The philosophe did not consider himself to be an ivory-tower individual dealing with abstract or abstruse questions. Although philosophy did involve thinking about intellectual matters, the task of a philosophe was to exert an influence on people who were not intellectuals. Voltaire's aim was to transform the often difficult treatises written by the more intellectually austere writers of the period into an effective weapon of propaganda (his expositions of Locke and Newton are classic examples of this). His own vigorous and witty style of writing, the very opposite of dry and dusty, was eminently suited to this enterprise.

Voltaire was certainly not unaware of serious philosophical problems, but he was also very much more aware of the inadequacy of the world he lived in. It is this which makes him a philosophe rather than a purely speculative thinker. To Voltaire the world around him appeared to display such a lack of reason and common sense that it was more important to transform it than to discuss anything more abstract: to adapt a phrase from Karl Marx, the important thing was to change the world and not merely to interpret it. Voltaire himself was basically a man of action who constantly complained that some of his fellow-philosophes – such as Diderot and, on occasion, d'Alembert – were spending too much time on the pursuit of their own pet lines of thought instead of being engaged in the work of agitation. Unlike contemporary thinkers such as Leibniz and Hume, he was rarely interested in purely speculative questions: nor did he concern himself with ideal solutions. This was what he thought Rousseau was doing, and consequently he despised him for it. However, his refusal to have any part in purely theoretical enquiries is not just a question of priorities, of the need for urgent and practical action: it stems fundamentally from a very deep-seated sceptical attitude. This basic scepticism is to be found everywhere in Voltaire's general approach. One of the principal tenets of his thought is that there are very few things that we can know for certain, particularly in matters which concern the ultimate meaning of things. Two consequences seemed to Voltaire to flow from this: firstly we should do all we can to reform the obvious wrongs that surround us; secondly, since we cannot be sure about absolute truths, we should not seek to impose our answers to imponderable questions on fellow human beings who may not agree with us. The only civilised stance therefore is one of tolerance, opposed to all forms of dogmatism. It is in terms of this outlook that the writings concerned with the Calas affair should be considered.

Religious controversy and persecution

Early on in his career Voltaire's reading of history had led him to conclude that the differences between religions constituted the single most important cause of strife in the world. While he welcomed the Reformation in sixteenth-century Europe because it challenged an authority based on revelation, he was equally opposed to the tendency of the reformed churches to replace this with the authority of the Bible, which seemed to him to be just as unacceptable (he was fond of retelling biblical stories so as to underline their flagrant disregard for the basic principles of morality). Furthermore, Protestants were quite as capable of barbarous fanaticism as their Catholic counterparts, even if the inhumanity shown to Candide by an intolerant Dutch minister does not match the horrors done to him by the Inquisition, and if the frequently mentioned execution of Servetus ordered by Calvin is hardly equivalent to the Massacre of St Bartholomew's Day in 1572. Voltaire was acutely aware of all the various acts of injustice and cruelty committed in the name of religion over the centuries from whatever quarter they emanated. His hatred of persecution, allied to an overall philosophy of scepticism, moved him inevitably towards a general hostility to most forms of organised religion. Such a view sets him apart from previous writers on the subject of tolerance, such as Bayle and Locke, whose firmly held Christian beliefs have little in common with Voltaire's own brand of religion – a deism that scorns ceremonies, rituals and particular articles of faith but makes a humanistic statement based on a belief in a providential order guided by a Supreme Being. Indeed the very multiplicity of the new spiritual denominations in Europe, let alone the existence of far older religious systems elsewhere, was for Voltaire sure proof that not one of them had the right to lay any claim to exclusive truth.

But Voltaire's arguments in favour of tolerance find their justification in events more recent than the Reformation. The whole climate of religious quarrels and persecution was one familiar to him from the declining years of the reign of Louis XIV in which he grew up. French prisons were full of Jansenists, victims of their devotion to a theology of divine grace that had been condemned by a papal bull (*Unigenitus*) secured from Rome by Louis XIV in 1713. Although the advent of the Regency in France heralded a relaxation of the pressure to eliminate the followers of Arnauld and Quesnel, the Jansenist party continued to be hounded well into the eighteenth century, and throughout the *Treatise on Tolerance* there are echoes of the prolonged struggle between the power of the state and this influential, deeply rooted religious sect. One example of the conflict may be seen in the reference to disturbances at Saint-Médard, a poor quarter of Paris, which led to the closure of its cemetery by the authorities in 1732 (ch. 5). Some years later tensions broke out on new ground: chapter 16 of the *Treatise* alludes to the decision by the archbishop of Paris to deny the last sacraments to those who could offer no proof that their confessor accepted the conditions of *Unigenitus*. They would be refused a Christian burial and thus would risk eternal damnation. The Paris parlement, with its strong Jansenist sympathies, took up the cause, which forced Louis XV into a protracted battle with the parliamentary faction on this issue. It was not until 1790, the second year of the French revolution, that the clergy were eventually granted civil rights in respect of worship.

Still more scandalous for Voltaire was the treatment meted out to French Protestants. The failure of the policy laid down by the Revocation of the Edict of Nantes, signed by Louis XIV in 1685, had become all too obvious in the eighteenth century. Despite reports of Calvinists flocking to the one true religion, the reality was very different. Conversions were either bought at an exorbitant price (Pellisson's activities on this front are graphically described by Voltaire in chapter 24), or they were extorted by brute force, the custom known as dragooning. A very great number of Huguenots fled the country: those unable to emigrate often formed pockets of unwelcome resistance, like the Camisards in the Cévennes whose rebellion (mentioned in chapters 10 and 12) had to be crushed at a time when France was hard pressed in defending its borders against foreign invasion. But lessons from the unfortunate consequences of this oppression were not drawn, for in 1724 the duc de Bourbon, Louis XV's prime minister, launched a new campaign against heresy. The old decrees were put into force once again: the death penalty for active Protestant ministers, and harsh sentences for their followers caught practising the cult. While the women were imprisoned for life, the menfolk were sent to the galleys. According to Antoine Court, whose book *Le Patriote français* confronts the question of Protestant loyalty, two hundred were condemned in this fashion in 1745 and 1746 alone, serving their time in the ports of Marseille and Toulon. And, on Voltaire's reckoning, eight ministers were hanged between 1745 and 1762.

Even if such spectacular punishment affected relatively few Protestants, all of them were subject to painful discriminatory measures. Their situation varied in different regions (Voltaire specifically mentions the more enlightened province of Alsace in chapter 4 of the *Treatise*), but in many parts of the country a Protestant had no official administrative existence, the legal fiction being that everyone was a Roman Catholic. Protestant marriages were not recognised, nor was the legitimacy of Protestant children unless their parents had been baptised by a Catholic priest. Burial was clandestine. Of course such conditions caused serious problems in matters of inheritance. It is interesting to note here that Jean Calas had been baptised and had married in a Catholic church (though not in Toulouse), had had his six children baptised as Catholics and had sent his four sons to a Jesuit school: yet the family, with the exception of one son, remained clearly Huguenot. Protestants were also excluded from a number of professions: the eldest Calas son had been prevented from becoming a barrister because he lacked the necessary certificate of catholicity.

Public worship, as has already been mentioned, was out of the question. In Paris it was possible for Protestants to attend services in the chapels of ambassadors of certain foreign powers (Holland, for example), though official spies noted down the names of those who took part. In the South, where in 1751 the bishop of Agen had publicly praised the Revocation of the Edict of Nantes and astonishingly denounced the 'loose morals' of the Calvinists, they met secretly in out-of-the-way places (the so-called churches of 'the desert'). This is the background to the horrifying case of Rochette, who was arrested at Caussade in September 1761 for carrying out his pastoral duties within the Huguenot assemblies. A French Protestant from Montauban named Ribotte wrote both to Voltaire and to Rousseau, begging them to intervene. Rousseau found himself in an awkward position: to defend Rochette would entail a plea based on universal freedom of conscience, which was quite unthinkable for anyone concerned – as Rousseau was – to uphold the cause of Calvinism in Geneva. Nevertheless he undertook to consider some form of action, and asked Ribotte to supply him with documentary evidence. In direct contrast Voltaire responded most perfunctorily. While Rousseau wanted to do something to help those he called 'our unfortunate brothers', Voltaire refers to them in a letter to the duc de Richelieu as 'wretched Huguenots', remarking cynically that Richelieu would become their idol if only he could manage to arrange Rochette's pardon. In February 1762 Rochette was hanged, and three brothers named Grenier, who had attempted to rescue him at the time of his arrest, were also executed (as noblemen they had the privilege of having their heads chopped off; given the alternative methods on offer at the time, this was indeed a privilege). Voltaire's biting comment was that they had been condemned for singing psalms because the Toulouse parlement disliked bad verse.

The Calas affair and the *Treatise on Tolerance*

Volatire's apparent flippancy about Rochette, on the very eve of the Calas case, is not simply attributable to his mischievous wit or a tendency to hide his sensibility behind a mask of irony. His reputation as someone who cared passionately about freedom of conscience was already well established, and for evidence of this we need look no further than Rousseau's letter on Optimism of 18 August 1756, which quite sincerely hails Voltaire as a fellow champion of tolerance. However, in the late 1750s Voltaire had, on various counts, become increasingly embroiled with the Genevan pastors, to such an extent that his relations with the city of Calvin were extremely strained. In eighteenth-century Geneva there was very little religious tolerance: as Voltaire had discovered personally (and this is mentioned specifically in his writing on the Sirven case), it was with great difficulty that Catholics could obtain permission to reside there; nor could they own any property. So his mood of irritation with the bastion of Protestantism helps to explain his rather hostile reaction to the appeal on behalf of Rochette.

Thus, on the level of practical politics, there could be a distinct coolness in Voltaire's approach to causes he might normally have been expected to defend. And a similar detachment is discernible in the initial stages of the Calas affair. It was barely four weeks after Rochette's execution that news reached Ferney of the fate of Jean Calas. He had been sentenced to death by the Toulouse parlement on 9 March and executed on the following day. The tone of Voltaire's first reaction is shockingly offhand: in a letter to Le Bault he compares Calas unfavourably to Abraham, with the conclusion that 'these Huguenots are worse than us, and furthermore they are against comedy'. Nevertheless a certain unease about the situation soon becomes evident. Whether Calas was guilty or not of killing his son, religious intolerance was involved, either on the part of bigoted Catholic judges or that of a fanatical Protestant father. Towards the end of March Voltaire wrote to a number of friends and acquaintances (Bernis, Fyot de la Marche, d'Argental, Chazel and d'Alembert) asking them to supply him with further information on the case, which is 'of vital interest to the human race'. Although he made repeated efforts to ascertain all the facts of the matter (including an interview with one of the Calas sons at Ferney), it did not take him long to make up his mind and be convinced of the innocence of Jean Calas. The beginning of what was to be a three-year campaign was announced in a letter to Damilaville on 4 April, in which Voltaire equates the affair with the horror of the St Bartholomew Massacre and signs off with the celebrated 'Cry it abroad and make others cry it too!' In the following months his correspondence bears all the marks of a steadily increasing obsession with the Calas family, which continued to preoccupy him until their final rehabilitation in March 1765.

In the summer of 1762 Voltaire composed a series of letters and memoranda, ostensibly from members of the family (the widow and the two sons Donat and Pierre), which were then published under the title *Pièces originales concernant la mort des sieurs Calas et le Jugement rendu à Toulouse*. The text on Elisabeth Canning belongs to the same period. Preparations for the *Treatise on Tolerance* itself seem to have begun in the late autumn of 1762, but some passages of the final version (notably the section on Germany in chapter 5) may have been drafted earlier, since they were originally intended for the tale *Pot-Pourri* and probably dictated in the spring of that year. The first mention of the *Treatise* occurs in a letter to Damilaville of 6 December, and its unfinished state is cited a few days later. A rough draft was ready by 2 January 1763, when Voltaire sent a copy of it to the pastor Moultou, asking him for his opinion of the work. Shortly afterwards he wrote again to Moultou, this time requesting a copy of Bayle's *Commentaire philosophique* and the bishop of Agen's letter against the Huguenots. Within a fortnight he appears to have reread Bayle's work, because he compares it with his own: 'his is long and abstruse. Mine is short and accessible to everyone.' After extensive revisions to the text, the second draft of the *Treatise* was completed by the end of January and sent to the printer Gabriel Cramer at the beginning of February with detailed instructions about the footnotes.

Although the *Treatise* was not finally printed until April, Voltaire was already making preparations for its circulation. He told Moultou that copies would be sent to Madame de Pompadour (the king's mistress), to some ministers of the privy council, and to a few chosen friends. It was also intended that the king of Prussia should receive a copy, along with other German princes who had taken an interest in the Calas affair. All remaining copies, however, were to be kept under lock and key until the right moment arrived for its general publication. These carefully laid plans about the book's destination, as well as the character of the work itself, reveal a great deal about the pragmatist in Voltaire. As in most matters, he was largely determined by what was likely to prove effective. Therefore a work of propaganda such as the *Treatise* would have to be witty and relatively brief, and it needed to be aimed, in the first instance, at persons in positions of influence, who were far more useful converts than the general public. Furthermore his fears about its premature release were not unfounded: when it was widely distributed after October 1763, court and government began to be alarmed, with the result that the book was officially banned. Voltaire was depressed by the prevailing lack of enlightenment in high places, looking forward to a time when 'the seed that has been sown will be able to germinate'.

A similar tactical sense is apparent in his handling of the Sirven case, which has many parallels with the Calas affair. Elizabeth Sirven, a convert to Catholicism, had been found dead in a well (not far from Toulouse) in January

1762. Her Huguenot family were accused of having murdered her, and a warrant was issued for their arrest. The father, mother and two daughters fled to Switzerland: in their absence the local judges sentenced all but one of them to death. Voltaire first mentions the Sirvens in a letter of 14 March 1763, expressing his fear that any action in their direction might harm the cause of Calas. From the start Voltaire knew that this case would be more difficult, because, as he put it ironically, 'unfortunately no one was broken on the wheel'. It was not until after the rehabilitation of Calas, two years later, that he judged it opportune to intervene, and the *Avis au public sur les parricides* [Address to the public concerning the Parricides imputed to the Calas and Sirven families], which links the two affairs, was finally printed in 1766. The campaign was a protracted one, Voltaire succeeding in obtaining an acquittal in 1771 and complete rehabilitation in 1775.

Far more sensational was the La Barre case, in which we see further evidence of the strength of the opposition and of the need to proceed with caution in France regarding matters of tolerance. By a strange coincidence Voltaire had just finished reading Beccaria's work on crime and punishment (on which he was to produce his own commentary in 1766) when he was offered a glaring example of brutal injustice. On the night of 6 August 1765 a wooden crucifix on the bridge at Abbeville was found mutilated, and two youths of eighteen, La Barre and d'Etallonde, were incriminated. D'Etallonde managed to escape, leaving La Barre to face the charges on his own. In February 1766, he was sentenced to have his right hand cut off and his tongue torn out, and to be burned alive. With minor modifications this was duly carried out on 1 July. Almost immediately Voltaire poured out all his indignation at the horrifying event in the *Relation de la mort du chevalier de La Barre* [An account of the death of the chevalier de La Barre], a work he was very cautious about circulating, awaiting a more favourable moment for its general distribution. In the trial the prosecution sought to prove that La Barre had been in possession of a number of impious and dangerous books, one of which was Voltaire's own *Philosophical Dictionary* (first published in 1764). Afraid for his own safety, Voltaire fled to Switzerland for a few weeks during the summer, conceding bitterly that 'there are times when you have to know how to keep silent'. This amounts to a reluctant admission of the limits of possible protest, given the prevailing political situation: 'I know only too well', he later remarked, 'that there are monsters you cannot tame. Those who steeped their hands in the blood of the chevalier de La Barre are people I would only wish to meddle with if I had ten thousand armed men behind me.'

While the La Barre case has nothing to do with the Protestant cause, it became firmly joined in Voltaire's mind to the other two affairs. He constantly referred to all three in the same breath, and we can view his most important writings of these years, in which he returns again and again to the issue of tolerance, as belonging to what he considered to be the same struggle against Christian persecution and superstition.

In the article 'Tolerance', which appeared in the first edition of the *Philosophical Dictionary* in 1764, Voltaire brings together several loosely connected strands of argument against Christian intolerance. Firstly he emphasises the theme of human weakness and the tendency to err, and claims that these should inspire us to humility and forbearance towards one another. The article shares this theme with the *Treatise* and with a work which deals with much wider philosophical issues, *The Ignorant Philosopher* of 1766. Secondly, the article suggests that the transactions of the stock exchange, although ostensibly merely utilitarian, in fact generate feelings of goodwill among those who participate in them, whatever religion they may belong to, comparing this unfavourably with the savage behaviour of Christians towards one another (Voltaire had touched on this line of argument earlier on in his career, in chapter 6 of the *Philosophical Letters* of 1734). Warming to its theme, the article then launches further attacks on Christian behaviour, concluding with the example of the massacre of St Bartholomew's Day. The *Treatise* had similarly detailed the oppressiveness of Christianity right down to the eighteenth century, contrasting this with the right-mindedness of Greeks, Romans and Hebrews (here Voltaire exonerates Moses, whereas in the *Dictionary* the same prophet is found guilty of the worst possible crimes!). Ever the practical thinker rather than the speculator, Voltaire draws freely on a variety of methods and arguments in support of his thesis – even a short story of the period, *L'Ingénu* of 1767, is partly adapted to the same campaign, with its picture of the incarceration of Jansenists and Huguenots. Fuelled by the cases of Calas, Sirven and La Barre, these works are all part of a war against bigotry and the miscarriage of justice. '*Ecrasez l'Infâme*' becomes Voltaire's war cry, and is to be found throughout his correspondence of the 1760s.

Natural religion, tolerance and society

Although Voltaire thinks that all organised religions are intolerant because they have stifled the voice of nature, he holds this to be especially true of the different branches of Christianity. In his poem 'On Natural Law' of 1752, he invokes for admiration the Prussia of Frederick the Great, which permitted all its inhabitants complete freedom in matters of cult and ceremony. Voltaire characterises this as 'indifference' and considers it to be one of the main reasons why people in Prussia can live in peace with one another. This idea enraged one critic of the poem, in whose orthodox opinion Voltaire was 'preaching the most scandalous tolerance and indifference to religion'. 'Indifference' is a key concept for Voltaire in this period and appears frequently in the letters relating to the composition of the *Treatise*, as he explicitly stresses a direct relationship between the progress of tolerance and the growing indifference to dogma – a theory which was, of course, bound to infuriate committed Catholics and Protestants alike. Voltaire's even-handedness extended to a warning, in this case to Protestants, that people can expect to be tolerated only if they are tolerant themselves (in his pamphlet *Remonstrances to the Pastors of Gévaudan*, 1768). For all this, Voltaire himself was not an atheist; his ideal citizen is the theist of the *Philosophical Dictionary* who scoffs at the idea of going on pilgrimages to Mecca or Notre-Dame de Lorette but who 'helps the needy and defends the oppressed'. Given that Voltaire is more interested in the conditions necessary for civil peace than in religious dogma, it is not surprising that his views diverge from those of his two main predecessors on the question of tolerance, John Locke and Pierre Bayle. Voltaire alludes to Locke in a short note at the start of chapter 11 of his *Treatise* when he claims that no citizen should be required to believe anything more than what his reason tells him. This point actually has more in common with Bayle's ideas than with Locke's.

Locke's main work on tolerance is the *Epistola de tolerantia*, which was published in 1689 but almost certainly drafted earlier. It was immediately translated from Latin into English, and later (1710) into French. By the mid eighteenth century it had been reprinted many times and had become something of a classic. Locke's letter was a very sober, scholarly piece, by no means directed at the wide audience which Voltaire intended to reach – with all his wit and emotion – in his campaign to mobilise public opinion. The political circumstances in which the two works were composed were very dissimilar. Locke was writing in exile in Holland, and addressing the situation in England under the Stuarts, just prior to the revolution of 1688 which drove out the Catholic James II – a monarch who was personally intolerant, and who, it was feared, would implement intolerant policies if he was allowed to continue in power.

One of Locke's central themes is the separation of religion from politics, of the Church from the State: 'I esteem it above all things necessary to distinguish exactly the business of Civil Government from that of Religion, and to settle the just bounds that lie between the one and the other.' The *Treatise on Tolerance* offers very little evidence of any thought along these lines. On the contrary, Voltaire, not unlike his contemporary Montesquieu, seems to view religion as an important means of cementing the social order and inspiring civic virtue. Provided that it is not fanatical, it can have a serious secular role to play. The opening paragraphs of chapter 20 are insistent on this: 'Mankind has always been in need of restraining influence . . . Wherever society is established, religion is essential.' The Church, Voltaire thinks, should be subordinated to the needs of the State, in such a way as to ensure a tolerant state of affairs. To Voltaire's way of thinking, the French Protestants' moderation of their more extreme demands (in particular he has in mind the holding of large outdoor assemblies) would be a fair price to pay for a more secure position within what was officially a Catholic country. In their turn, the more bigoted Catholics would be held firmly in check by the power of government or, more precisely in France, by royal authority. Thus in strictly political terms Voltaire's position is quite distinct from Locke's separation of powers, in that he was favouring a solution that included a state religion, whereby an established church would have the confidence to allow, to a limited extent, non-conformist tendencies; this would have the effect of defusing sectarian hatreds.

What is noteworthy about the *Treatise* is the moderation of the position it takes. The petition which Voltaire makes in chapter 5 is an extremely limited one: peace-loving Protestants should be allowed to live undisturbed lives to the extent that the 'validity of their marriages should be acknowledged', while 'their children should enjoy security and the right to inherit from their fathers'. In other words, the civil rights denied to them by the Revocation of the Edict of Nantes would be restored. Significantly there is no mention here of freedom of worship – quite the contrary, since there are to be 'no public temples'. The implicit analogy is with the position of Catholics in England, which Voltaire had witnessed in the 1720s; like the English Catholics, French Protestants would not have access to public offices or honours. Voltaire's hopes, on a purely practical level, appear to have been that a dissident minority could be accommodated in the same way that the Anglican Church ('the faith in which one prospers', as he sarcastically remarked in the fifth Philosophical Letter) permitted a plurality of sects – the existence alongside it of Quakers, Presbyterians and Socinians.

Voltaire's extreme theoretical moderation was equalled by the political prudence with which he conducted his dealings with the king's minister Choiseul during the 1760s, in an attempt to bring about a policy of toleration. Even these very limited demands for reform, however, were not met in the years immediately following 1763. Certainly in the wake of the Calas affair a far less harsh attitude towards Huguenots prevailed, but there were no changes to the law itself. Only in 1787 did Louis XVI promulgate an edict of tolerance that restored civil rights to Protestants, despite having appointed Necker, a committed Calvinist, as his First Minister ten years earlier.

At first sight the similarity between Bayle's thought and Voltaire's is very striking. Principally they share a common scepticism, derived in Bayle's case from his own sufferings as a Protestant driven, like Locke, into exile in Holland. His famous work *Commentaire philosophique sur ces mots de Jésus-Christ, contrains-les d'entrer* (1686) is often considered to be the main source of the French Enlightenment's ideas on tolerance, and was reread by Voltaire as he drafted his *Treatise*. Like Locke's *Epistle*, it is more academic in style than Voltaire's text.

More important, there is a basic difference of approach between the two writers. Bayle treated faith as a matter of profound inner conviction, and the whole of his argument in favour of tolerance was organised around the inviolable rights of individual conscience. So thoroughgoing is he in this respect that he seems to accord a place to atheists, traditionally feared by eighteenth-century philosophers as a threat to the social order. Indeed the logic of his argument could lead to an acceptance of the persecution of those of another persuasion, if conscience so demanded. He was aware that this sort of conclusion might be drawn, for he added that such a state of mind should be opposed by more enlightened reasoning. Nevertheless, in the final analysis he emphasises the overriding value of belief (or non-belief) as something that no external authority should have the power to challenge. In stark contrast to this, Voltaire's most usual attitude towards the details of Christian belief, in both the *Treatise* and his other writings, is one of unrestrained sarcasm. He refers mockingly to petty disputes about the Holy Trinity (chapter 11) and about the Logos (chapter 21). While he follows Bayle in examining in detail a famous parable from Saint Luke (chapter 14), his criteria for evaluating it are very different from those of his predecessor – they are much more external and secular. What is of greatest value for him, as he clearly states at the end of the fourth chapter, is 'the physical and moral well-being of society'. Tolerance is necessary in the 'political interest of nations'.

The whole agenda has therefore changed from a religious to a social one. Voltaire and his contemporaries may have been regressive when compared with Bayle on the matter of individual conscience, but they were surely progressive in the sense that their arguments against persecution were no longer formulated in terms of traditional Christian concepts, nor was their case for tolerance being made within a strictly Christian framework. Voltaire widens the angle of vision in the *Treatise on Tolerance* and gives us a world view of the human race embracing a multitude of beliefs: 'Let us reach out of our narrow little sphere and examine what goes on in the rest of the globe' (chapter 4). A similar spirit of internationalism is evident in the closing stages of the work. Chapter 22 is significantly entitled 'On Universal Toleration', and in the following chapter, 'A Prayer to God', there is a vibrant plea for co-operation among mankind. This is a fitting conclusion to the book, so that the postscriptum together with its sequel and an addendum come as something of an anticlimax, although Voltaire may have deemed it necessary to provide a progress report on the Calas affair with which he had started out.

Voltaire's brand of optimism may well strike us, two and a half centuries later, as naïve and misplaced, but there is no doubt that his ideas continue to strike chords with us. Poignantly, in chapter 4 in a passage about atrocities committed in Ireland, he stated that they could never happen again, but his analysis of parades and processions in mid-eighteenth-century Toulouse, designed to incite hatred against a minority of the population, is both pertinent and disturbing. The twentieth-century experience of religious and political fanaticism has led to renewed sympathy with Voltaire's humane plea for general tolerance in the public realm. Barthes might have been right to suggest that Voltaire was fortunate to be fighting in a just cause and, by implication, that his cause was better than his arguments, yet there is no doubt that he has made an immense contribution to our understanding of the causes and effects of prejudice.

Chronology

1766	Dedicates his account of the death of the chevalier de La Barre to Beccaria. Publishes *Le Philosophe ignorant*
1767	Publishes *L'Ingénu*
1778	Returns to Paris, where he dies on 30 May

Further reading

There are three great editions of Voltaire's writings: the so-called Kehl edition, edited by Beaumarchais and others, *Œuvres complètes*, 70 vols. (1785–89); *Œuvres*, edited by A. J. O. Beuchot, 72 vols. (1829–40); and *Œuvres complètes*, edited by Louis Moland, 52 vols. (1877–85). Moland's edition, based on Beuchot's scholarship, has long been the vulgate, but a new *Complete Works* with full critical apparatus is now being published by the Voltaire Foundation in Oxford (1969–). It will eventually comprise more than a hundred volumes. Equally extensive is Theodore Besterman's edition of Voltaire's correspondence (1953–65). An edition of the *Treatise on Tolerance* itself, which is likely to become the standard one, has been prepared by John Renwick and is due to be published by the Voltaire Foundation in 2000 (*Complete Works*, 56B). In the meantime a briefer edition by Renwick is available in paperback (Vif, 1999). Accompanying it in the same series is a useful collection of essays on the *Treatise* edited by Nicholas Cronk.

Some of Voltaire's other important works have also been published in separate critical editions. For example, Gustave Lanson's exemplary, fully annotated two-volume edition (1909, reprinted several times) should be consulted for the *Lettres philosophiques*. But Voltaire's original text of this in English, entitled *Letters concerning the English Nation*, has recently been issued in the World's Classics series with an excellent introduction by Nicholas Cronk. There are also good English translations of the *Philosophical Dictionary* and of *Candide* in the Penguin Classics series. Of similar interest to English readers are the editions of the *Traité de métaphysique* (H. Temple-Patterson), *Zaïre* (E. Jacobs), *Zadig* (H. Mason), *Candide* (J. Brumfitt), *L'Ingénu* (W. R. Jones) and *Le Philosophe ignorant* (J. L. Carr), all of which contain very scholarly introductions. Mention must also be made of D. Williams, *The Political Writings of Voltaire* (1994), which gives the complete text of the Commentary on Beccaria in English translation. This is a seminal piece for Voltaire's thinking on crime and punishment.

The fullest and most up-to-date account of Voltaire's life and works is a huge five-volume opus, *Voltaire en son temps* (1985–94), edited by René Pomeau. Rather more manageable, and still a standard work, is the same scholar's provocatively entitled *La Religion de Voltaire* (1956). Even more approachable is Haydn Mason, *Voltaire: A Biography* (1981), an authoritative piece by a leading English specialist on Voltaire. Also highly recommended is Peter Gay, *Voltaire's Politics* (1959), which, as its title implies, concentrates on his social attitudes and his campaigning efforts. Gay's bibliographical essay at the end of the volume is especially rewarding.

On the particular question of religious toleration the most comprehensive study is probably to be found in Graham Gargett, *Voltaire and Protestantism* (1980), which has a detailed discussion of Voltaire's involvement with Dutch, English and Swiss reformers as well as a lengthy treatment of the Huguenot movement in France. David Bien, *The Calas Affair* (1959), offers a useful corrective to the Voltairean view of persecution in eighteenth-century Toulouse from a modern historian's perspective. In terms of the history of ideas there have been a number of important contributions in recent years: *Voltaire, Rousseau et la tolérance* (Amsterdam, 1980); Elizabeth Labrousse, 'Note à propos de la tolérance au XVIIIe siècle', *Studies on Voltaire*, 56; R. A. Leigh, *Rousseau and the Problem of Tolerance* (Oxford, 1979); and S. O'Cathasaigh, 'Bayle and Locke on Toleration', in *De l'humanisme aux lumières*, ed. M. Magdelaine et al. (Oxford, 1996). For a general evaluation of the topic by philosophers in our own century, see the collective volume *A Critique of Pure Tolerance*, ed. Robert Wolff (London, 1969), which includes a typically combative essay by Herbert Marcuse.

Note on the texts

Many of Voltaire's works deal with the question of tolerance, but from 1762 onwards it becomes one of his key themes. The publication of the *Treatise on Tolerance* is closely bound up with Voltaire's involvement in the Calas affair that year: if we quote the full title in French we see that the work is directed against a specific evil; indeed the *Traité sur la tolérance à l'occasion de la mort de Jean Calas* begins and ends with the famous case. Other writings concerning the affair both precede and follow the *Treatise*: of these I have included the piece *The Story of Elisabeth Canning and the Calas Family*, produced in August 1762 as a polemic to stir up opinion abroad, and the *Address to the Public concerning the Parricides imputed to the Calas and Sirven Families* (printed in 1766), which, while more immediately concerned with the Sirven affair, uses the Calas trial as well to make its point. While these two texts, like the *Treatise on Tolerance*, were translated into English soon after their original appearance, a new version is called for to make them accessible to the modern reader.

A third affair was to follow closely on those of Calas and Sirven, that of the chevalier de La Barre. Voltaire's powerful *Account of the Death of the Chevalier de La Barre*, composed in 1766 and dedicated to the marquis de Beccaria, is published here in its first full English translation, together with the companion piece, *The Cry of Innocent Blood*, produced nine years later in defence of La Barre's friend who had escaped to Prussia.

These four relatively short brochures help us both to broaden our understanding of the *Treatise on Tolerance* and to fit it into its immediate context. The *Treatise* itself – started in the autumn of 1762, completed in January 1763, and printed in April but not circulated until later that year – was translated into English soon after its publication in France. The translation by Brian Masters used here, which was originally published by the Folio Society, was commissioned to coincide with the tercentary of Voltaire's birth in 1694. The text translated by Masters is the one which first appeared in the second volume of the

Nouveaux mélanges in 1765, when Voltaire added a final chapter to celebrate the clearing of Jean Calas. It is this text, together with the author's original footnotes, which is presented in the most readily available of current French editions (*L'Affaire Calas*, ed. J. Van den Heuvel, Folio, 1975; *Traité sur la tolérance*, ed. R. Pomeau, Garnier-Flammarion, 1989).

The translation of the title *Traité sur la tolérance* calls for some comment. Since the eighteenth century this has usually been given as *A Treatise on Toleration*, in conformity with Locke's *Letter on Toleration*, which was published in English in 1689–90. In the French language there is no specific term to denote religious toleration as such, and Voltaire himself refers to Locke's work in a footnote as the *Lettre sur la tolérance*. In the present volume the word 'tolerance' has been used throughout, in chapter headings and in the main body of the text, in preference to 'toleration'. It not only possesses a more modern ring, but also corresponds more closely to Voltaire's wider concern with individual liberty and with the more general issues of freedom of thought and speech.

Treatise on Tolerance

I
A brief account of the death of Jean Calas

The murder of Calas, sanctioned by the sword of justice on 9 March 1762, in the city of Toulouse, is one of the most extraordinary events to claim the attention both of our own age and of posterity. The masses of corpses fallen in numberless battles are apt quickly to be forgotten, not only because such fatalities are inevitable in war, but also because those who perish by force of arms might as easily have killed their enemy, and in no sense died without the opportunity to defend themselves. When danger and advantage meet in equal measure, there is less cause for astonishment, or even pity. But if the innocent father of a family is delivered into the hands of prejudice, or ignorance, or fanaticism; if, once accused, he has no other defence but his good character; if those who control his fate run no other risk, in putting him to death, than that of making a mistake; if they may kill by decree with impunity; then public opinion is outraged and each man fears for himself. As soon as we realise that no one's life is secure before a tribunal which was established precisely for the protection of us all, the entire population must rise in unison to demand vengeance.

At issue in this remarkable affair were religion, suicide and murder; whether a father and a mother had strangled their own son in order to please God; whether a brother had killed his brother, a friend his friend; and whether magistrates had cause to reproach themselves for having condemned an innocent father to death on the wheel, or, on the other hand, for having spared a guilty mother, brother and friend.

Jean Calas, aged sixty-eight, had been a merchant in Toulouse for more than forty years and was acknowledged by all who had lived with him to be a good father. He was a Protestant, as were his wife and all his children, save one who abjured the heresy and to whom he made a small allowance. So far removed was he from that absurd fanaticism which ruptures all the bonds of society that not

3

only did he approve the conversion of his son Louis Calas, but he had entrusted the care of all his children to a servant who was a devout Catholic.

Another of his sons, Marc-Antoine by name, was a man of letters. He was known to be broody, saturnine, and prone to violence. Having failed to enter into business, for which his personality was not suited, or to be received at the Bar, because he was unable to obtain the necessary certificates of catholicity, this young man resolved to end his life, and gave some indication of his intention to one of his friends. He further strengthened his resolution by reading everything that had ever been written on the subject of suicide.

At length, having one day lost money at the gambling table, Marc-Antoine decided to put his design into effect. One of his friends was the nineteen-year-old son of a famous Toulousain lawyer, an open-hearted and sweet-natured youth called Lavaisse; he was also a friend of the family. Lavaisse had arrived from Bordeaux the night before[1] and was, by chance, dining with the Calas family that evening. The company included the parents, Marc-Antoine, the eldest son, and Pierre, the second son. After dinner they retired to a small drawing-room and Marc-Antoine absented himself. Some time later, when young Lavaisse desired to leave, he and Pierre Calas went downstairs and there found Marc-Antoine, in shirt and breeches, hanging from the door of the storeroom. His coat and waistcoat were neatly folded on the counter. His shirt showed no signs of disorder, his hair was well combed, and there was not a mark or bruise upon his body.[2]

We shall pass over some of the details of which the lawyers have given sufficient account. Nor shall we describe the grief and despair of the parents, whose lamentations were heard by neighbours. Lavaisse and Pierre Calas, beside themselves with terror, ran to fetch a surgeon and a magistrate.

While they were about this, and while the parents were racked with weeping, the people of Toulouse gathered outside the house. They are a superstitious and hot-headed race, who regard as nothing short of monstrous those of their fellow men who follow a different religion from their own. It was in Toulouse that solemn thanks were offered to God for the death of Henri III, and that oaths were sworn to cut the throat of any man who dared recognise the great and good Henri IV. It is in Toulouse that processions and bonfires still mark the anniversary of the day, two centuries ago, when four thousand heretics were massacred.

---

[1] 12 October 1761. [Voltaire's note]

[2] The only marks found on the body after its removal to the town hall were a tiny scratch on the end of the nose and a small bruise on the chest, no doubt caused by carelessness when carrying it. [Voltaire's note] There were folding doors between the shop and storeroom. The young man had placed a heavy rod across the top of the door and hanged himself from that. It was contended that suicide was not feasible, because the rod would not hold and the man's feet would anyway touch the ground, but some local boys re-enacted the death and proved it possible; no matter how much they squirmed and shook, the rod did not give way.

4

In vain have six Orders in Council prohibited this odious festival; the people of Toulouse have continued to treat it as a celebration.

Some fanatic or other in the crowd shouted out that Jean Calas had murdered his own son, and within no time the cry became unanimous. Others added the information that the deceased had been due to recant the following day and that his family and Lavaisse had conspired together to strangle him out of hatred for Catholicism. The rumour immediately became a certainty. The whole city was persuaded that it was an article of faith among Protestants for parents to slaughter their offspring if ever they evinced a desire to convert.[3]

Once passions like these are aroused it is impossible to contain them. Word soon got about that the Protestants of Languedoc had assembled the night before and had selected one of their number, on a majority vote, to be executioner; that the choice had fallen upon young Lavaisse; and that, within twenty-four hours of the receipt of this news, he had travelled from Bordeaux in order to assist Jean Calas, his wife and their son, in the murder of their son and brother, and his friend – Marc-Antoine Calas.

Upon hearing these reports, a *Capitoul*[4] or Senior Magistrate of Toulouse, Sieur David, immediately recognised an opportunity to advance his reputation by prompt action and thereupon initiated a prosecution contrary to all custom and precedent. He had the Calas family, the Catholic servant and Lavaisse all arrested and placed in irons.

He caused a Monitory, no less defective than the prosecution itself, to be published.[5] He went even further. Marc-Antoine Calas died a Calvinist; had he committed suicide, his body should have been dragged through the streets in

---

[3] The belief that Protestants were required to murder their recusant sons derived in part from Calvin himself, who had written in his *Institution de la religion chrétienne*: 'All those who resist the authority of a father, whether through lack of respect or through rebellion, are monsters and not men. For this reason our Saviour has ordered us to put to death all those who disobey father or mother.' On the other hand, Marc-Antoine was so far from being a potential convert that it was he who habitually led the family in prayer.

[4] The *Capitoul* was a title peculiar to Toulouse, given to municipal magistrates of that city from the Middle Ages until the Revolution. Each district of Toulouse provided its own *Capitoul*, the total number varying at different times between four and twelve. They were not usually men versed in law, and dealt only with minor offences such as disorderly conduct. Sometimes, however, growing too powerful and too self-satisfied, they usurped the functions of the higher-court judges in parlement; the Calas affair was one such instance.

[5] Sponsored by the Church, a Monitory was an effective means of finding witnesses to a crime. It was first read out from the pulpit and then posted up, and it demanded that anyone with material information should come forward. The law required that it should be scrupulously impartial, and should not name a suspect who might still be innocent. The Monitory in the Calas case was first read out on 18 October, five days after the death of Marc-Antoine, then repeated on 25 October and 8 November. It was disgracefully biased, assuming in every article that Marc-Antoine had been murdered by his family. There followed a Fulmination, which threatened anyone withholding information with instant excommunication. This produced only hearsay and innuendo. There never was any evidence against Jean Calas.

shame. And yet he was interred with great pomp in the church of St Etienne, in spite of the priest's objections against such profanation of sanctified ground.

In Languedoc there are four brotherhoods of penitent – the white, the blue, the grey and the black. The friars wear a long cowl with a woollen hood pierced with two holes for the eyes. They had ambitions to enlist the Governor of the Province, the Duke of Fitzjames himself, among their number, but he declined the honour. The white friars accorded Marc-Antoine Calas the most solemn obsequies, as befitted a martyr. Never had any church celebrated the feast of a true martyr with greater display. Yet there was something dreadful about this ceremony. Above a magnificent catafalque they placed a skeleton, which they contrived to move and jerk. It bore in one hand a palm, and in the other a quill. The skeleton represented Marc-Antoine Calas, the quill the instrument of his supposed recantation; except that it signed instead the death warrant of his father.

This unfortunate suicide lacked only the glory of canonisation. The entire populace considered him a saint; some invoked his name; others prayed on his tomb; still others besought him to work miracles, or told of those he had already accomplished. A monk tore some teeth from the corpse as relics. A devout but somewhat deaf woman declared she could hear the sound of bells. An apoplectic priest was cured after taking an emetic. Official reports on these wonders were commissioned and duly written. The present writer has in his possession an affidavit to the effect that a young man of Toulouse lost his sanity for having prayed several nights in a row on the tomb of the new saint without procuring the miracle for which he craved.

Some of the magistrates belonged to the fraternity of the white penitents, a fact which may well have rendered the death of Jean Calas inevitable.

His fate was sealed by the approach of that odd festival which the Toulousains celebrate annually to commmemorate the massacre of four thousand Huguenots; 1762 was the bicentenary.[6] When the trappings for this solemn ritual were erected in the town, they further worked upon the already over-heated imaginations of the populace. It was publicly stated that the scaffold upon which the Calas family would perish was to be the festival's most glorious ornament. It was said that Providence herself had delivered these victims to be sacrificed unto our most sacred religion. Twenty witnesses overheard these utterances, as well as others yet more violent in tone. And this in our own day! In an age when Enlightenment had made such progress! When a hundred academies have devoted their energies to the promotion of decency and gentleness in public affairs! Fanaticism, infuriated by the advance of Reason, is thus seen to thrash about in an agony of frustration and renewed spite.

---

[6] The massacre referred to here took place ten years before the massacre of St Bartholomew, i.e. in 1562. The victims were unarmed and singing psalms.

Thirteen judges assembled every day to hear the case for the prosecution. There was no evidence against the family, nor could there be, so injured religion was served up instead. Six of the judges were obdurate in demanding the wheel for Jean Calas, his son and Lavaisse, and the stake for his wife. The seven others, more moderate, thought that at least the defendants might be heard. Debate was long and laboured. One of the judges, convinced both that the accused were innocent and the crime impossible, argued warmly in their favour; against the passion of intolerance he opposed the zeal of his humanity. He became the public defender of the Calas family in all those households where religious fervour, feeling itself threatened, clamoured for the blood of these wretched people. Another judge, of harsh reputation, harangued the citizens against the Calas family with as much vigour as the former showed eagerness in their defence. The scandal was finally so great that they were both obliged to disqualify themselves from the case and withdrew to the country.

By a most unfortunate chance, however, while the judge who had defended Calas observed the restraint imposed upon him, the other resumed his attacks against people he no longer had a right to condemn. It was his voice which was eventually responsible for the sentence of death, for there were eight votes against five, but one of the judges in favour of acquittal, at the last moment and after much dispute, switched his vote to the harsher faction.

In a case of parricide, when it might be necessary to condemn the father of a family to the most appalling agonies, it seems right that the verdict should be unanimous, because the proofs of so outlandish a crime[7] must be derived from evidence which may satisfy everyone and anyone; the slightest doubt in such a case must be sufficient to stay the trembling hand of any judge poised to sign the death warrant. The fragility of our reason and the inadequacy of our laws are daily made manifest; what more terrible instance could be offered than the sight of a man being broken alive on the wheel on the strength of a single casting vote? The citizens of Athens required a straight majority plus fifty votes before they permitted themselves to pass sentence of death. And what do we learn from that? Only the bootless reflection that the Greeks were wiser and more humane than we are.

---

[7] I know only two instances in history of fathers being charged with killing their children on account of religion. The first is the case of the father of St Barbara. He had had two windows made in his bathroom. Barbara, in his absence, had a third made to honour the Holy Trinity. She made the sign of the cross on the marble columns with the tip of her finger, and it was deeply engraved on the stone. Her father came angrily upon her, sword in hand; but she escaped through a mountain which opened to receive her. The father went round the mountain and caught her. She was stripped and flogged, but God clothed her in a white cloud. In the end her father cut off her head. So says the *Flower of the Saints*. The second case is that of Prince Hermengild. He rebelled against his father, the king, engaged him in battle in 584, was defeated and killed by an officer. As his father was an Aryan, he was regarded as a martyr. [Voltaire's note]

7

It was clearly impossible that Jean Calas, an old man of sixty-eight who had long suffered from weak and swollen legs, should have strangled and hanged his son of twenty-eight, whose strength, moreover, was above the average; it would have been absolutely necessary for him to be assisted in the crime by his wife, by his son, Pierre, by Lavaisse, and by the servant. Besides, on the evening of the fatal event they had not left each other's side for one moment. Yet this latter proposition is as absurd as the first. For how could one conceive that an ardent Catholic servant should suffer Huguenots to assassinate the young man she had brought up all his life, precisely to punish him for embracing the religion she herself professed? How could it be imagined that Lavaisse should make the journey from Bordeaux expressly to kill his friend when he was totally ignorant of his supposed conversion? How could one suggest that a tender-hearted mother should stain her hands with the blood of her own son? And how did one suppose that they could join forces to strangle a young man who was more robust than all of them put together, without a long and violent struggle, without screams to alert the entire neighbourhood, without blows, bruises or torn clothing?

It was obvious then, if the murder were to be at all possible, that all the accused must be equally guilty because they had not separated all evening; it was obvious that they were not guilty; it was obvious that the father alone could not be guilty; yet despite all this, the father alone was condemned to be broken on the wheel.[8]

The grounds for this sentence were, like all the rest, quite beyond belief. The judges who had determined that Jean Calas should die managed to persuade the others that this feeble old man, being unable to withstand the torture, would break down and confess his crime and that of his accomplices. They were therefore somewhat abashed when he, with his dying breath, summoned God as witness to his innocence and asked that His forgiveness be extended to his misguided judges.[9]

---

[8] The sentence, which was never made public, was divided into four parts: (1) that Jean Calas be subjected to the Question, both ordinary and extraordinary, until he confess his crime and his accomplices; (2) that he should be taken barefoot in a cart to the cathedral and make *l'amende honorable* before the hangman, asking forgiveness of God and the King; (3) that he should then be taken to the scaffold, where his arms, legs, thighs and loins would be broken; (4) that he should finally be laid upon a wheel with his face to the sky to spend his last hours in pain. The Question Ordinary consisted in slowly stretching the victim; the Question Extraordinary involved suffocation, the victim's nose pinched while great quantities of water were poured through a funnel into his throat. Records show that Jean Calas withstood this torment without once submitting to the torturers' threats, and consistently denied that any crime had taken place.

[9] Eye-witness accounts agree that Jean Calas met his end with extraordinary heroism. As his limbs were broken he let out one cry with each blow, but was otherwise serene and calm. On the wheel his cracked bones mingled with the spokes, yet still he resisted bitterness or recrimination. He would not ascribe his sentence to wickedness or religious fanaticism; the magistrates had been misinformed, he said. David de Beaudrigue (Sieur David), beside himself with anger and obviously assailed by doubts, shouted at Calas to confess, but to no avail. Two hours after being

Thus did they find themselves obliged to pass a second sentence which contradicted the first, according to which they set free the mother, Pierre Calas, Lavaisse and the servant. When it was pointed out to them that this new decision invalidated the other; that they had thereby passed judgement upon themselves and stood condemned; that, as all the defendants had remained together throughout the time of the alleged murder, the release of the survivors proved beyond doubt the innocence of the one who had been executed, they then made the decision to send Pierre Calas into exile. This banishment was as inconsistent and absurd as everything that had preceded it, for Pierre Calas was clearly either guilty or innocent of the murder; if guilty, he should have been broken on the wheel like his father; and if innocent, he should not be banished. The judges were so taken aback by the father's agony and the touching piety with which he died, that they thought to save their honour by showing mercy to the son, not realising that their display of mercy was, at that point, yet another miscarriage of justice. No doubt they thought that it was a matter of little consequence to send an impoverished young man into exile without support of any kind, and being unimportant, was but a tiny injustice compared with those they had already had the misfortune to commit.

They visited Pierre Calas in his cell and threatened to treat him as they had his father, unless he renounced his religion. The young man has testified to this on oath.[10]

As he was leaving the city, Pierre encountered a priest specialising in conversions who obliged him to return to Toulouse, where he found himself locked up in a Dominican monastery and forced to observe all the customs of the Catholic faith. Part of their objective in so doing was to make him avenge their religion as the price of his father's blood; religious feeling was thereby appeased.

The daughters were then taken from their mother and likewise locked in a convent. As for this wretched woman, who had been virtually bathed in her husband's blood, who had held the body of her eldest son in her arms and seen another sent into exile, who had been robbed of her daughters and stripped of all her goods, she was now quite alone in the world, without subsistence or hope and almost dead with the weight of her misery. Now there were certain persons who, bringing mature examination to bear upon this frightful affair, were so struck by the horror of it that they pressed the widow Calas to emerge from her solitude and demand justice from the King himself. She was, by this time, in no state to comply, being weak and drained by her experience. Besides which,

---

placed on the wheel, he was manually strangled in a gesture of mercy, a pitiful but noble sight to all who were present, many of whom had known and respected him for forty years.

[10] 'A Dominican monk came into my cell and threatened me with the same manner of death unless I abjured. This I attest before God, 23 July 1762. Pierre Calas.' [Voltaire's note]

having been born in England and moved to a French province at an early age, the very name of Paris struck fear into her heart. She imagined that the capital of the kingdom must be even more barbarous than Toulouse. But in the end her sense of duty towards the memory of her husband overcame her fragility. When she eventually arrived in Paris she was close to death, and amazed to find herself greeted with warmth, succour and sympathy.[11]

Reason is more powerful than Fanaticism in Paris, whereas in the provinces it is generally Bigotry which prevails.

M. de Beaumont, the celebrated lawyer of the Paris Courts of Justice, was the first to champion her cause; he drew up a legal opinion to which fifteen of his colleagues put their signatures. The no less eloquent M. Loiseau prepared a statement on behalf of the family. M. Mariette, advocate of the Council, composed a judicial paper on the case which carried universal conviction.

These three noble defenders of justice and innocence surrendered to the widow all profit from the published editions of their views.[12] Not only Paris, but the whole of Europe was moved to pity by her plight and joined her in demanding justice. Thus was public opinion notably in advance of the actual signature in Council which would restore common sense.

Compassion reached even to the seat of government despite the perpetual press of business which often must exclude it, and despite also that familiarity with misfortune which can harden the heart still further. The daughters were soon reunited with their mother, and all three, dressed in mourning, wept before their saviours.

Nonetheless, this family still had enemies. Why? Because religion was involved. Several of those people known in France as *dévots*[13] loudly proclaimed that it was better an old Calvinist, albeit innocent, should die on the wheel than that eight councillors of Languedoc should be obliged to admit that they were in error. It was even said that 'there are more magistrates than Calases', the inference being that the Calas family should be sacrificed to preserve the honour of the judiciary. These people did not reflect that the honour of judges, like that of other men, lies in correcting their mistakes. No one in France believes that the Pope, assisted by his cardinals, is infallible;[14] it might be fair to suggest that

11 It was said Mme Calas was received by both Mme du Deffand, Walpole's friend, and Mme de Geoffrin, and she was eventually presented to the Queen. From across the Channel messages of support came from the Archbishop of Canterbury and no fewer than twelve dukes.

12 Since the texts were pirated in many towns, the widow Calas did not receive the benefit intended by this act of generosity. [Voltaire's note]

13 *Dévot* comes from the Latin *devotus*. The *devoti* of ancient Rome were those who sacrificed themselves for the good of the Republic, such as the Curtii or Decii. [Voltaire's note] In France the word came to signify passionate dedication to faith and carried a pejorative connotation.

14 The doctrine of papal infallibility was not defined until 1870 at the Vatican Council. Voltaire refers to the more general belief in the freedom from error which St Peter and his successors enjoyed, as Bishops of Rome, by the action of divine grace.

neither are eight judges of Toulouse. Sensible, unprejudiced men declared that the Toulouse verdict would be quashed anywhere else in Europe, notwithstanding that there might be special circumstances to prevent its being overturned in Council.

Such was the state of affairs in this astonishing story when certain impartial and sensitive persons conceived the notion of presenting before the public some reflections on tolerance, on clemency, on compassion, those values which the Abbé Houtteville,[15] in an inflated and misinformed harangue, recently called a 'monstrous dogma', and which men of Reason affirm to be the natural prerogatives of Humanity.

Either the magistrates of Toulouse, led astray by the fanaticism of the populace, have caused an innocent man to perish on the wheel – which is without parallel; or the man and his wife squeezed the life from their eldest son, aided and abetted in this appalling act by another son and his friend – which is against nature. In either case, the abuse of the most holy religion has resulted in a terrible crime. It is therefore in the interest of mankind to examine whether the true religious spirit is more consistent with charity or with cruelty.

[15] Claude-François Houtteville (1686–1742), author of *La Vérité de la religion chrétienne prouvée par les faits* (1722), which was widely criticised and had to be seriously revised for its second edition in 1740. Houtteville taught ecclesiastical history at Tours and became secretary to Cardinal Dubois.

2

On the consequences of the execution of Jean Calas

If, in fact, the white penitents have caused an innocent man to be executed, an entire family to be ruined, split up, and treated with that contempt which ought to be reserved for the authors of injustice, but is frequently piled upon its victims; if these white penitents, in their haste to canonise a young man whom they ought more properly (in accordance with our barbarous customs) to have dragged through the streets in shame,[16] thereby caused the torture and death of a virtuous father; then such a calamity ought well and truly to make both them and their friends the magistrates repent for the rest of their lives, and not with the protection of a long white habit to hide their identity, nor a mask to conceal their lamentation.

The religious brotherhoods are held in high esteem for their contribution towards the education of our people; but however great their benefit to the State, can it compensate in any degree for the terrible evil they may cause? Their very foundations appear to be built upon that extremism which, in Languedoc, so manifestly excites Catholics against those whom we call Huguenots. You would think they had made a vow to hate their fellow man, for though we have in our country sufficient religious feeling to revile and persecute, it is not yet strong enough to love and to cherish. And where on earth would we be had these fraternities been governed by enthusiasts like those who, in former times (so at least according to one of our most eloquent and learned magistrates), used to run establishments where the habit of seeing visions was elevated to an art form and a discipline? What would happen if our fraternities were to adopt special dark rooms, called *meditation chambers*, the walls of which they would daub with

[16] Suicides in Toulouse were stripped naked, placed face downwards on a hurdle and paraded through the streets for spectators to hurl mud and stones at. Then the body was hung from a gibbet and the property of the dead man confiscated.

horned and clawed devils, flaming chasms, crosses, daggers, and the sacred name of Jesus inscribed above the whole lot? What a sight to behold for eyes already wide with wonder and for imaginations, being abjectly obedient to their controllers, already worked into a frenzy!

We know only too well that there was a time when these fraternities were downright dangerous. The Floggers and the Flagellants were the cause of much mischief, and the Catholic League in effect arose from such beginnings.[17] Why should these men have sought to distinguish themselves from other citizens thus boldly? Did they deem themselves to be superior, perfect? If so, that in itself was an insult to the rest of the country. Or did they want every Christian to enter a brotherhood of monks? What a pretty sight that would have been, the whole of Europe clad in hoods and masks with two little round holes to peep through! Do they really think God prefers such an outfit to a plain jerkin? Worse than that, this clothing acts as partisan uniform to warn adversaries they should be on their guard; it could provoke a kind of spiritual civil war which could lead to the most pernicious excess, were the wisdom of the King and his ministers not equal to the madness of the fanatics.

We know, too, what has been the cost of Christians disputing over dogma: blood has flowed aplenty, both on the scaffold and on the battlefield, from the fourth century right up to our own day. We shall confine ourselves here to the wars and horrors which followed on the Reformation in France, and look into their causes. We must hope that a brief and honest account of so many calamities might open the eyes of the ignorant, as it will touch the hearts of the good.

---

[17] The Catholic League was founded by the duc de Guise in 1576 to protect the Catholic Church against the encroachments of Calvinists, or Huguenots, and more especially to prevent the accession of the Protestant Henri de Navarre to the throne of France. It was supported by Philip II of Spain and Pope Gregory XIII. Its declared policy was to uphold the religious integrity of the nation against incompetent or misguided kings, but since two other prominent officers of the League were the duc de Cayenne and the Archbishop-Cardinal of Rheims, both brothers to the duc de Guise, it was suspected that a concealed purpose might be to acquire the throne for the Guise family itself.

3
A sketch of the reformation in the sixteenth century

When the Renaissance ushered in the beginnings of enlightenment, there were sore complaints that it was accompanied by some abuses; no one now disputes that these complaints were justified.

Pope Alexander VI had openly purchased his crown, and his five bastard sons divided the spoils which accrued therefrom. One of them, Cardinal the Duke of Borgia, in concert with his father the Pope, put to death the Vitellis, the Urbinos, the Gravinas, the Oliverettos, and the families of a hundred other noblemen, in order to seize and plunder their lands. Julius II, moved by similar ambitions, excommunicated King Louis XII and offered his throne to first-comers, while he himself, in helmet and full armour, devastated a good part of Italy. Leo X, in order to finance his pleasures, trafficked in pardons as one sells turnips in the market. Those who protested against such outrages could scarcely be faulted from the moral point of view. Let us see whether, from the political, they were quite so wise.

The reformers pointed out that, since Jesus Christ had never demanded *annates* or looked for reversions,[18] nor sold pardons in this world and indulgences for the next, there was no cause why they should give the price of these things to a foreign prince. If we calculate that, with the initial fees, the law-suits in Rome, and the dispensations which continue to this very day, the cost to us is five hundred thousand francs a year, it is clear that in the two hundred and fifty years since François I we have paid out one hundred and twenty-five millions: taking into account the difference in the value of money, this is equivalent to about two hundred and fifty millions in today's currency. One might well advance the proposition therefore, without risk of blasphemy, that the heretics

---

[18] *Annates*: when Roman Catholic bishops and clergymen were appointed to a see or benefice, they surrendered the first year's worth of their revenue to the Pope.

who sought to abolish these quaint taxes, which will doubtless astonish posterity, did no disservice to the kingdom, and would be better reckoned good
mathematicians than bad subjects. We should add that they alone understood
the Greek language and were familiar with the ancient world. Let us honestly
acknowledge that, despite their mistakes, it is to them that we owe the progress
of human understanding, which had for so long been buried beneath an
impenetrable barbarism.

But since they denied the existence of Purgatory, which was of course an
indubitable fact and, moreover, one very remunerative to the monks; since they
refused to worship relics, which of course one should worship, for they were
even more profitable; since, finally, they dared to attack the most revered
dogmas,[19] our immediate response was to burn them. The King, who was
supposed to be their protector and kept a body of them in pay in Germany,
marched at the head of a procession in Paris, the culmination of which was the
public execution of a number of these unfortunate wretches. The execution
proceeded in the following manner: they were suspended from the end of a
see-saw, a long beam pivoted in a tree in a manner to enable it to be lowered and
raised; beneath them was lit a great fire; they were then plunged into the fire, and
hoisted up again alternately, thus being made to experience torment and death
by lingering degrees until such time as they expired. It was the most protracted
and excruciating ordeal ever devised by barbaric ingenuity.

Shortly before the death of François I, the priesthood in Provence became
excited against the inhabitants of Mérindol and Cabrières and persuaded some
members of their parliament to petition the King for troops to assist the arrest
and execution of nineteen peasants whom they had condemned to death. In the
event, they murdered six thousand, sparing neither women, children nor the
elderly, and they reduced thirty villages to ashes. These countryfolk, until then

[19] They repeated the opinion of Berengarius on the Eucharist: they denied that a body could exist in
a thousand different places at one and the same time, even by the intervention of divine power;
they denied that attributes could exist without a subject; they believed it was absolutely
impossible that that which was to the eyes, to the palate, and to the stomach, simple bread and
wine, could have its essence abolished at the very moment of its existence; in a word, they
maintained all those errors for which Berengarius had been condemned. They based their
teaching on several texts written by the early Fathers of the Church, above all those of St Justin
who says in his *Dialogue against Tryphon*: 'The presentation of bread to God in the Eucharist is
what Jesus orders us to do in memory of his passion.' They recalled all that had been written in
the first centuries of the church against the workship of relics, citing these words of Vigilantius:
'Can it be necessary for you to revere and even adore a piece of contemptible dirt? Can the souls of
the martyrs still be attached to their ashes? The customs of idolatry are now introduced into the
Church, where tapers are lit at noon. We may pray for each other while we are alive, but what is
the purpose of praying for the dead?' But they did not quote St Jerome against this passage in
Vigilantius. In short, they wanted a return to the times of the apostles and did not acknowledge
that, as the Church grew in size and strength, it had had to extend and fortify its discipline. They
condemned the magnificence which seemed necessary, however, to support the dignity of
religious worship. [Voltaire's note]

quite unknown to the rest of the world, were obviously grievously at fault for having been born in the Vaud, but that was their only crime. They had established themselves three hundred years earlier on barren and mountainous terrain which they had rendered fertile by superhuman effort. Their pastoral, idyllic life recalled the uncluttered innocence of primeval times. They only visited neighbouring towns in order to sell their fruit; they knew nothing of law-courts or wars; they did not bother to defend themselves; they were slaughtered like animals in a pen.[20]

After the death of François I, a prince better known for his dalliance and unhappiness than for his inhumanity, the victims of this escalating persecution were so incensed first by the murder of a thousand heretics, and especially that of Counsellor Dubourg, and then by the massacre of Wassy, that they took up arms.[21] Meanwhile, by the light of the faggots and under the blows of the executioners, their numbers had multiplied. Patience gave way to anger. They copied the cruel practices of their enemies. Nine civil wars covered France in blood. A peace yet more deadly than any of the wars produced the carnage of St Bartholomew, a crime without equal in the annals of man's wickedness.[22]

The Catholic League assassinated Henri III and Henri IV, the first by the

---

[20] Madame de Cental, who owned some of this ravaged land, now littered with the corpses of its inhabitants, appealed to Henri II for redress. He referred her to the Parliament of Paris. The Attorney-General of Provence, a man called Guérin, who was principally but not solely responsible for the massacre, was the only one condemned to lose his head, for, says de Thou, he had no friends at court and thus took all the blame himself. [Voltaire's note] The sack of Mérindol and Cabrières took place in 1545 on the order of the Parliament of Aix. Forces under the command of Baron d'Oppède massacred all the inhabitants without exception.

[21] Wassy in the Haute-Marne had been a royal residence under the Merovingian monarchs. On Sunday 1 March 1562, François de Guise was passing through when a quarrel broke out between his men and some Protestants who were holding a prayer meeting in a barn. In the ensuing mêlée, sixty Protestants were killed and over two hundred wounded. This incident was the spark for civil war throughout the whole of France. Wassy was pillaged by the Catholic League in 1591.

[22] The massacre of St Bartholomew, so called because it began in Paris on St Bartholomew's Day, 24 August 1572, was an attempt by Catherine de' Medici to wipe out the entire Huguenot party at one go. The daughter of Lorenzo de' Medici, she had been born in Florence and married Henri II of France. Her three sons became kings of France – François II, Charles IX and Henri III – and she was regent during the minority of Charles IX, over whom she continued to exercise considerable influence. Her power was, however, threatened by the opposing influence of Admiral Coligny, whom she therefore determined to have assassinated. The attempt failed, but it infuriated the Huguenots, who had flocked to Paris for the wedding of Henri de Navarre and were restless. Catherine held a meeting in council with the Catholic leaders, at which the solution was reached, and she persuaded her son the King that the massacre was necessary for public order and safety. He gave his assent on the evening of 23 August. The murders began at dawn the next day, continuing in Paris for three and a half weeks. They spilled over into the provinces, where they went on unabated until 3 October, though some provincial governors refused to authorise them. In all about 50,000 people died. Catherine de' Medici was congratulated by the Catholic powers, and Pope Gregory XIII commanded bonfires to be lit in celebration and a commemorative medal to be struck. The massacre unleashed the fourth war of religion in France, and Charles IX died overcome with remorse.

hands of a Jacobin monk, the second by a monster who had belonged to the order of *Feuillants*.[23] There are some who claim that humanity, tolerance and freedom of thought are terrible things; but, in all conscience, could they have produced catastrophes worse than these?

[23] The Jacobin monk who murdered Henri III in 1589 was Jacques Clément; with his dying breath the King named Henri de Navarre as his successor; Henri IV was assassinated in 1610 by a fanatic called Ravaillac. The *Feuillants* originally belonged to the Abbey of Citeaux, until Pope Sixtus V granted them independence in 1586 and they formed their own separate order. By 1768 they had expanded to twenty-four houses throughout France and 162 monks, but at the Revolution their order was abolished, they were dispersed and their property was confiscated.

4

On whether tolerance can be dangerous, and in which countries it is permitted

There are some who maintain that, were we to treat with friendly forbearance those errant brothers of ours who pray to God in bad French, we should be guilty of placing weapons in their hands and encouraging them to replay the battles of Jarnac, Montcontour, Coutras, Dreux, Saint-Denis and so on. I cannot say, for I am not a prophet. But there seems to me a want of logic in the argument which proposes, *These men rose up in arms when we treated them badly; therefore they will rise up in arms when we treat them well.*

I shall now take the liberty of inviting those who sit at the head of government, together with others destined for high office, to join me in a mature examination of the following questions: Are we justified in believing that tolerance might excite the same revolutionary spirit as has been provoked in the past by persecution? Are events which occurred under certain circumstances bound to be repeated in others? Do customs, opinions, habits, never change?

It is beyond doubt that the Huguenots have been as drunk with fanaticism and steeped in blood as the rest of us. But is the present generation as barbaric as its predecessors? Have not the age in which we live, the progress of Reason, the fine literature we enjoy and the gentle manners we promote, reached to the men who instruct the minds of these people? And have we not noticed that practically the whole face of Europe has changed over the last fifty years or so?

Everywhere government has become stronger and society gentler. Police forces, supported by extensive regular armies, ensure that we need not fear a return of those anarchic times when Calvinist peasants fought Catholic peasants in scratch militias put together between seed-time and harvest.

A new age must bring new attitudes. It would be absurd to punish the Sorbonne today for having in the past petitioned to burn Joan of Arc, or declared that Henri III forfeited his right to reign, or excommunicated and banished the great Henri IV. Just as ridiculous would it be to root out those other establishments once guilty of excess in times of madness. Such would not only be unjust, it would contain about as much sense as to subject the entire population of Marseilles to a wholesale medical cure today because they had been visited by the plague in 1720.

Are we about to sack Rome, as did Charles V and his troops, because, in 1585, Pope Sixtus V granted nine years' worth of indulgences to every Frenchman who took up arms against his sovereign? Is it not enough to prevent Rome from falling into such excess ever again?

The fury unleashed by both the dogmatic spirit and the misuse of a poorly understood Christianity has spilt as much blood and caused as many disasters in Germany, in England, and even in Holland, as in France. However, religious differences present no problem today in those countries; the Jew, the Catholic, the Greek Orthodox, the Lutheran, the Calvinist, the Anabaptist, the Socinian, the Mennonite, the Moravian and many others, live there as brothers and contribute equally to the good of society.

In Holland there is no longer any fear that the arguments of a Gomar[24] on the subject of predestination should cost the old man his head. In London they no longer worry that quarrels between Presbyterians and Episcopalians over liturgy and surplice could lead a monarch to the scaffold and spill royal blood. In Ireland, newly populated and enriched, there will be no repeat of those scenes of Catholic citizens sacrificing Protestant citizens to God for two whole months, burying them alive, hanging young mothers from the gallows with their daughters strapped to their necks so as to watch them die together, splitting open the bellies of pregnant women and pulling out half-formed babies to throw to dogs and pigs to eat, placing a dagger in the hand of their garrotted prisoners and guiding the dagger into the breasts of their wives, fathers, mothers, daughters, with the depraved intent of creating parricides by this device and thus not only exterminating them all, but sending them all to Hell. Such is the testimony of Rapin-Thoyras, an officer serving in Ireland roughly at the time of these events;[25] so, too, testify all the annals and histories

---

[24] François Gomar was a Protestant theologian who, in contradiction of his colleague Arminius, maintained that God had predestined the greater part of mankind to burn eternally in Hell-fire. This infernal doctrine was upheld, naturally, by persecution. The Grand Pensionary of Holland, Barneveldt, who disagreed with Gomar, had his head severed on 13 May 1619, at the age of seventy-two, 'for having done his best to annoy the Church of God'. [Voltaire's note]

[25] Paul de Rapin's *Histoire d'Angleterre* in eight volumes was virtually the only history of the country available in France during the first half of the eighteenth century, so Voltaire would have known it well.

of England covering the period. It can never happen again, for Philosophy, that is the only true philosophy, the sister of Religion, has now disarmed hands so long bloodied by superstition, and the human spirit, as it recovers from its toxic madness, stands astonished at the excesses to which bigotry once brought it.

We have in France a wealthy province where Lutheranism carries more popular support than Catholicism. The University of Alsace is in the hands of the Lutherans, who occupy several municipal offices of government as well. Never once has the slightest religious dispute disturbed the peace of this province ever since it has been part of our kingdom. Why? Because it has never been contaminated by persecution. Seek not to enslave hearts, and all hearts will be yours.

I do not say that all those who profess a different religion from that of the reigning prince should share in the places and honours available to those who are of the prevailing religion. In England, Roman Catholics are considered as belonging to the party of the Pretender, and are therefore denied office; they even pay double tax; yet they still enjoy all other privileges of the citizen.

A few French bishops are rumoured to think that it would serve neither their honour nor their interest to permit Protestants to live in their diocese, and this obduracy is said to be the greatest single obstacle to tolerating them. I cannot believe it. The great majority of bishops in France are from distinguished families – they think and act with a dignity worthy of their ancestry; one must give them credit for their innate charity and nobility of mind; they must surely reflect that their persecuted sheep, seeking refuge in foreign parts, are unlikely to be converted there, whereas they could be enlightened by the wisdom and example of their pastors once they returned to the fold; there would be honour in converting them, with no harm to their temporal rights; and the more sheep there are, the better it is for episcopal coffers.

A bishop of Varmy, in Poland, had a farmer who was an Anabaptist and a tax-collector who was Socinian. He was advised to throw out the one, on the grounds that he did not believe in the doctrine of consubstantiality, and the other, because he did not baptise his son until the boy was fifteen years old. He replied that though they would both surely be damned to eternity in the next world, in this one they were still very useful.

Let us reach out from our narrow little sphere for a moment, and examine what goes on in the rest of the globe. The Turkish prince, for example, rules peacefully over twenty races of different religious conviction; two hundred thousand Greeks live in Constantinople in perfect safety, and the Mufti himself nominates and presents the Greek patriarch to his emperor; there is even a Roman Catholic patriarch living there. The Sultan nominates Catholic bishops to some of the Greek islands, with the following words: *I commend him to go and reside as bishop on the isle of Chios in accordance with its ancient customs and vain ceremonies.* This empire is stuffed with Jacobites, Nestorians, Monothelites, Coptics, Christians of St John, Jews, Gebers and Banians. The annals of Turkey bear no record of a revolt raised by any of these religious communities.

Go to India, to Persia, to Tartary, and you will find the same evidence of tolerance and mutual respect. Peter the Great gave his protection to every possible cult in his vast empire, to the benefit of both agriculture and commerce and with no detriment whatever to the body politic.

For more than four thousand years the rulers of China have adopted only one religion, which proclaims the simple worship of one God.[26] On the other hand, they tolerate the superstitions of Fo,[27] as well as a multitude of Buddhist priests who could be dangerous had they not always been contained by sensible legislation.

It is true that the great Yung-Chin, perhaps the wisest and most magnanimous emperor that China has ever known, expelled the Jesuits. However, that was not because he was intolerant, but rather because they were.[28] In their *Lettres curieuses* the Jesuits themselves related the words with which this good prince addressed them: 'I know that your religion is intolerant. I know what you did in the Manilas and in Japan. You deceived my father. Do not expect to deceive me as well.' To read the whole speech which he graciously made to them is to be convinced of his sagacity and clemency. How could he, after all, have allowed European philosophers to remain at court when, under the pretext of demonstrating thermometers and eclipses, they had already once made off with a prince of the blood royal? What, I wonder, would this emperor have said, had he read our European history and known all about the Catholic League and the Gunpowder Plot?

It was enough that he should be informed of the squalid quarrels between Jesuits, Dominicans, Franciscans and secular priests, sent into his domains from the other end of the world to preach the truth and who spent their time cursing one another. The Emperor did no more, then, than to send packing some foreign trouble-makers. But with what display of kindness! Such paternal attention was there lavished on the preparation of their journey home and such great care

---

[26] More properly, the ancient faith of China did not worship one God as a powerful ruler and creator; rather did it acknowledge the notion of a Supreme Being, who was pleased by virtue and upset by wickedness.

[27] A Chinese Buddha.

[28] Yong-Tcheng (1677–1736), Emperor of China from 1723 to 1736 of the Manchu dynasty. He was son of Emperor Kanghi, who added Tibet to the empire and welcomed the Jesuit missionaries. According to Catholic sources, Yong-Tcheng persecuted Jesuits.

taken that they should escape insult along the way! Their banishment was itself a supreme example of tolerance and humanity.

The Japanese were the most tolerant of all nations. Twelve peaceful religions were already established within their empire when the Jesuits came to add the thirteenth. It was soon apparent, however, that these cared little for competition and proceeded to suppress the others. We know what ensued. A civil war, no less terrible than those of the Catholic League, devastated the country. The Christian religion finally drowned in its own oceans of blood; the Japanese closed their empire to the rest of the world once and for all, deeming us to be no better than wild animals, like those of which the English had purged their island. Minister Colbert was keenly aware that we needed the Japanese far more than they needed us, but it was in vain that he pleaded for trade links. He found them to be utterly inflexible.

And so the history of our entire continent gives proof that it is foolish either to promulgate religious intolerance or to base policy upon it.

Cast your eyes across the Atlantic and take a look at Carolina, whose legislation was framed by the philosopher John Locke. There you need only seven heads of families to establish a religion approved in law, a freedom which has contrived to ferment no disorder whatever. God forbid we should cite this example as one which France should emulate! We bring it forth only to demonstrate that one may push the principle of tolerance to its furthest extreme without exciting the slightest public disturbance; we must allow, however, that what is good and useful in a nascent colony may not be suitable in an ancient kingdom.

And what shall we say of those simple folk, somewhat derisively known as *Quakers*, whose customs are perhaps ridiculous but whose virtuous behaviour has shown the rest of the world, uselessly as it turns out, the meaning of Peace? There are a hundred thousand of them in Pennsylvania. Discord and controversy are unknown in the happy homeland they have made for themselves. And the very name of their city of Philadelphia, which reminds them constantly of the brotherhood of man, is both an example and a reproach to those nations who have yet to learn tolerance.

In the end, tolerance has been responsible for not a single civil war, whereas intolerance has covered the earth with corpses. Let us therefore judge between these two opposing figures, between the mother who would have us slay her son, and the mother who will part with him in order that he may live.

I refer here only to the political interest of nations. And, respecting as I must the tenets of theology, I do not intend to deal in this essay with anything more than the physical and moral well-being of society. I implore every impartial reader to weigh these truths, to correct or expand them. By sharing their thoughts on these matters, readers will penetrate more deeply than the author can.[29]

[29] M. de la Bourbonnaie, the intendant of Rouen, says that the manufacture of hats at Caudebec and Neuchâtel has greatly declined on account of the expatriation of the Huguenots. M. Foucaut, the intendant of Caen, says that trade in the region is barely half what it used to be; and M. de Maupeou, intendant at Poitiers, tells us that the manufacture of druggets has entirely ceased. M. de Bezons, in Bordeaux, tells us tht there is hardly any trade at Clérac and Nérac. M. de Miroménil, the intendant of Touraine, says that the commerce of Tours has diminished by ten million livres per annum, and all this on account of religious persecution. (See the memoirs of the intendants for 1698.) Add to this the great number of officers on land and at sea, as well as the common sailors, who have been obliged to serve the enemies of France, frequently with fatal consequences for their own country, and then judge whether or not religious persecution has been destructive to the State. We will not presume to offer any advice to those ministers whose conduct and capacity are sufficiently well known, and whose greatness of mind and nobility of sentiment do honour to their illustrious birth; they will readily perceive that the restoration of our navy will require some indulgence to be shown to the inhabitants of our coasts. [Voltaire's note]

5
To show how tolerance may be permitted

I venture to imagine that perhaps an enlightened and magnanimous Minister of State, or a humane and wise priest, or a prince who can recognise that his interest is identical with that of the majority of his subjects, and that his glory lies in their happiness, might deign to cast a glance at this crude, imperfect essay of mine; that he might compensate for its defects with wisdom of his own; that he might say to himself, 'What risk would I run, in seeing my land better cultivated with more manpower, my revenues increase, my State flourish the more?'

Germany would now be a desert covered with the bones of Catholics, Evangelicals, Reformers and Anabaptists, all massacred by each other, were it not for the Peace of Westphalia[30] which eventually established in that country the right to freedom of thought.

We have Jews in Bordeaux, in Metz, in Alsace; we also have Lutherans, Molinists, Jansenists in other parts of our country; could we not suffer the Calvinists to live among us, contained by more or less the same conditions as apply to the Catholics living in London? The more sects there are, the less dangerous each one becomes; as they multiply, so they weaken; and all are held in check by fair laws which prohibit tumultuous assembly, public insult and

---

[30] The Treaty of Westphalia, signed on 24 October 1648, was in fact two treaties negotiated simultaneously, between the German empire and France on the one hand, and the empire and Sweden on the other, and it brought an end to the Thirty Years' War. The provisions of the treaty included much territorial adjustment, France gaining Alsace, for example, and recognition of sovereignty over Metz, Toul and Verdun, Sweden receiving western Pomerania and Bremen, and acquiring control of the Baltic. Central authority in the empire was reduced, and that authority vested in local princes was enhanced. Most important, equality of tolerance was recognised for all three major religious communities, with specific reference to freedom of private worship, of conscience and of emigration. The Protestant minority in the Imperial Diet was not to be coerced by the Catholic majority, and religious disputes were thenceforth to be settled in sober discussion.

incitement to sedition, laws which are kept in force by the consent of the people.

It is known that there are many heads of families who have made great fortunes in foreign countries and are now desirous of returning to their homeland. They ask only that they be accorded the protection of natural law, that the validity of their marriages be acknowledged, that their children should enjoy security and the right to inherit from their fathers, that they be given proper sanctuary. They ask for no public temples, no charge upon the public purse, no honours; Catholics already enjoy none of these things in London, nor in many other Protestant countries. Nobody is suggesting that we bestow immense privileges and sinecures upon a particular faction, only that we allow a peace-loving people to live unmolested, and that we soften the effect of edicts which were once perhaps necessary, but are no longer so. It is not for us to tell the minister what he should do. We can but beseech him on behalf of these unfortunate people.

There are many ways of making them useful and preventing their ever becoming a danger to the State. The minister and council with their customary good sense, allied to the exercise of military power, will soon discover these methods, already employed with happy results in many other countries.

There exist still some fanatics among the Calvinist population; but it is evident that there are far more among some Catholics, witness the 'convulsing' sect of Jansenists.[31] While the insane human dregs of St Médard are held of little consequence, the Calvinist madmen,[32] on the other hand, are ruthlessly annihilated. The one sure method of diminishing the number of these lunatics, should there be any left, is to expose their mental disease to the influence of Reason, the one slow but infallible route towards enlightenment. Reason is gentle, humane, tolerant; she smothers discord, strengthens goodness, and renders obedience to the law so attractive that coercion is no longer necessary to uphold it. And we should not lightly dismiss the derision with which all educated persons now-adays view the subject of religious enthusiasm. Such derision is a powerful barrier to inhibit the bigots from going too far. Past eras must be treated as if

[31] The Jansenists were a French sect named after the Dutch theologian Cornelius Jansen (1585–1638), who taught that no amount of church-going could save a man unless the love of God was in him, and that only God could decide whether to bestow His love. Jansenism presented itself as a development of St Augustine's theory of grace. It established a hold at Port-Royal and gave rise to much intellectual debate with the Jesuits, who heartily disapproved of its harsh doctrines. Louis XIV did not approve of the Jansenists' claim to independent authority and persuaded Pope Clement XI to act against them. The result was the papal bull *Unigenitus*, which appeared to condemn virtually anything a Catholic might do of his own volition. The Jansenists fled France, leaving a rump of increasingly fanatical followers. The Convulsionaries worked themselves into a state of apoplectic frenzy by means of terrible self-inflicted tortures and claimed to cure diseases and make prophecies in such a state, presumably because madness took them closer to God. They were suppressed by the police, but were still active at the time Voltaire was writing his *Treatise*, for Diderot deplored their influence in 1772.

[32] Voltaire is referring to the revolt of the Camisards in the Cévennes, which started in 1702.

they had never been. One must always start from the present, from the point to which nations have thus far evolved.

There was a time when men felt obliged to prosecute those who taught against the categories of Aristotle, against the notion that nature abhors a vacuum, against metaphysical quiddities, or against what logicians call objective universals. In Europe we can boast more than one hundred volumes of statutes dealing with sorcery and with how to distinguish a true witch from a false one. Grasshoppers and other insects harmful to our crops were routinely excommunicated, and in some rituals they still are. But the practice itself has disappeared; we now leave Aristotle, witches and grasshoppers in peace. Examples abound of such idiocies, which were once treated with the most solemn seriousness; others still occur from time to time; but when they have achieved their effect, that is when one has had one's fill, they evaporate. If anyone today were to announce himself a Carpocratian,[33] or a Eutychean,[34] or Monothelite,[35] Monophysite, Nestorian,[36] Manichaean,[37] or goodness knows what else, what would happen? We should laugh ourselves silly, as if we had just spotted a man dressed in doublet and hose.

Our country began to open its eyes when the Jesuits Le Tellier and Doucin fashioned their bull *Unigenitus*, and sent it to Rome;[38] they thought they were still living in times of ignorance, when people believed anything they were told, no matter how absurd. They dared denounce the proposition, which is universally true in every case and at any time, that *Fear of an unjust excommunication must in no circumstances prevent a man from doing his duty*. In other words, they

[33] Carpocrates was a Gnostic of the second century AD, whose followers held that morality was internal, and that external behaviour was therefore a matter of indifference. They were consequently among the most notoriously licentious of all sects. The Carpocratians further maintained that Jesus was born of normal human parentage.

[34] Eutyches, a presbyter at Constantinople at the beginning of the fifth century, opposed the Nestorians and held that Christ was not two natures, the human and the divine, but one nature – the incarnate Word.

[35] In the fierce debates which occupied the Church during the seventh century, the Monophysites maintained that Christ had only one nature, and their successors, the Monothelites, that He had only one will.

[36] Nestorius was Patriarch of Constantinople from 428 to 431, and the Nestorian heresy which bears his name developed from his idea that Christ was two natures combined in one.

[37] Mani, born in 216 to Iranian parents in a Jewish-Christian community in southern Mesopotamia, proposed a new universal religion in opposition to the teachings of Buddha, Christ and Zoroaster. He evolved a system of ethical and spiritual duality of great complexity, but which was based on the simple notion that all the good of the world came from light, and all the evil from the darkness which surrounded it. The world of light had God at its head, whereas Satan derived from the world of darkness, and was also eternal. This idea attempted to fuse Christian theology with a materialistic pagan view.

[38] Michel Le Tellier (1643–1719) was appointed confessor to Louis XIV on the death of Father La Chaise. It was he who persuaded the King to destroy Port-Royal, the Jansenist stronghold.

Louis Doucin (1652–1721) was one of Le Tellier's few confidants. A fanatically committed Jesuit, he helped Le Tellier push through the papal bull *Unigenitus*.

proscribed Reason, the liberties of the French Church, and the foundations of morality. They were saying, in effect, that God orders us never to do our duty if we are afraid we may meet with injustice as a result. Never has common sense been so monstrously affronted. The doctors of Rome were caught unawares and failed to recognise this truth. Persuaded that the bull was necessary and that the French nation desired it, the court at Rome permitted it to be signed, with consequences we now know. Surely, had they been anticipated, the bull would have been toned down. There were loud disputes on the matter, and only the goodness and prudence of the King managed to appease them.

The same is true of a good many points which distinguish the Protestants from ourselves; some of them are of no importance whatever; others, to be sure, are more grave; but the passions they once aroused have become so cool that not even the Protestants themselves bother to mention them in the course of their sermons.

This age of disgust with the past, this age of satiety and the triumph of Reason, this will be the era of public harmony. The dread epidemic of controversy has run its course; we are now cured of this particular plague and ask to be fed on a milder diet. It is in the interest of the State that exiled sons should be allowed to return, with humility, to their fathers' hearths; humanity demands it, Reason counsels it, and politicians need not be afraid of it.

6
On intolerance as natural law or human right

Natural law is that which nature demonstrates clearly to all men. You have brought up your child; he therefore owes you respect as his father and gratitude as his benefactor. You have the right to harvest the products of land you have cultivated with your own hands. You have both given and received a pledge, and that pledge must be honoured.

A human right can only be founded upon this Natural Law, and the great principle which governs both the one and the other throughout the world is this: *Do unto others as you would have done unto yourself.* Now, following this principle, there is no way a man may say to another, *Believe that which I believe and you cannot believe, or you will die.* Yet that is precisely what they do say in Portugal, in Spain and in Goa. In some other countries today they limit themselves to saying, *Believe, or I shall hold you in abhorrence; believe, or I shall do you all the injury of which I am capable; monster that you are, if you have not my religion, then you have none; you are obliged to be an object of hatred to your neighbours, to your city, to your province.*

Were it a human right to behave in this manner, then the Japanese would have to detest the Chinaman, who would in turn need to execrate the man from Siam; he would then persecute those who live by the Ganges, who would fall upon others who live on the Indus; a Mongol would tear to pieces the first Hindu he could find, the Hindu could slay the Persian, who could massacre the Turk; and the whole pack would hurl themselves at the Christians, who have already spent so long in devouring each other.

The right to persecute is therefore absurd and barbaric; it is the law of the jungle. Nay, it is yet worse, for wild animals kill only to eat, whereas we have exterminated one another over a parcel of words.

7
On whether persecution was known to the Greeks

History teaches us that all peoples, including those of whom we have but little information, have ever considered their various religions as links in a chain which bound them together, echoes of their common humanity and descent. There existed a kind of hospitality among gods as among men. Should a stranger arrive in town, his first duty was to worship the local deity; one never failed to venerate the gods even of one's enemy. The Trojans, for instance, prayed to the gods who were fighting, supposedly, on behalf of the Greeks.

Alexander went off to the Libyan desert to consult the god Ammon, to whom the Greeks gave the name *Zeus* and the Romans *Jupiter*, although they both had their own Jupiter and Zeus back at home. When armies besieged a city, it was their custom to offer sacrifices and prayers to the gods of that city in order to win their favour. Thus, even in the thick of war, religion acted as a unifying force among men and, occasionally, a mollifying stay upon their ferocity, as well as commanding them at times to commit the most appalling brutalities.

I could be mistaken, but it seems to me that not one of the civilisations of the ancient world inhibited freedom of thought. They each had a religion, but I have the impression they used it with regard to men in much the same way as they did with regard to deities, that is to say, they all recognised a Supreme Being, while allowing Him a prodigious quantity of inferior gods as lieutenants; or they maintained one religious concept, while permitting it a host of individual expressions.

The Greeks, for example, despite being religious, were perfectly happy that the Epicureans should deny both Providence and the existence of the soul. Not to mention all the other sects, whose ideas insulted the very notion of a

Creator, and yet who were each allowed to worship in their way without hindrance.

Socrates came closer to an understanding of the Creator than any of the ancients, and he paid the price by dying a martyr to his discovery: he remains the only person the Greeks ever killed for his opinions. If such was in fact the reason for his downfall, it does no credit to the spirit of intolerance, because they punished the one who alone gave glory to God, yet they covered with honour all those whose ideas of the Divinity were among the most crass. The enemies of tolerance ought not, in my view, to claim for themselves the odious example offered by those who sat in judgement on Socrates.

Besides which, it is clear that he fell victim to a furious cabal ranged against him. He had made irreconcilable enemies of the sophists, the orators and the poets, all of whom taught in the schools, and even of the private teachers employed to guide the sons of noble families. He himself admitted, in a dialogue reported by Plato, that he had gone from house to house exposing the pretensions of these teachers as the baldest ignorance. Such behaviour was hardly worthy of a man whom an oracle had declared to be the wisest on earth. They sent a priest and a councillor of the Five Hundred to accuse him – I confess I know not of what precisely, for his own *Apology* is vague on the subject; he was generally said to have incited the young with dangerous ideas against religion and government. This is the method of calumniators the world over and in all ages. But a court of law should have to deal with attested facts and the accused should face a precise and detailed indictment. This was emphatically not the case in the trial of Socrates. We know only that he started with two hundred and twenty votes in his favour. The Council of the Five Hundred contained, therefore, two hundred and twenty philosophers. That is quite a lot. I doubt whether we should find as many in any other tribunal. In the end the majority were for death by hemlock. Let us remember, however, that when the Athenians realised what had happened, they held the prosecutors and judges in contempt; Meletus, the prime mover for conviction, was himself condemned to death, and the rest were sent into exile. There was even a temple erected in memory of Socrates. Never had philosophy been so well avenged, nor so brilliantly honoured. In the last analysis, the example of Socrates presents the most conclusive argument of all against persecution. The Athenians dedicated altars to foreign deities whom they could not possibly know. Has there ever been a more powerful example, not only of tolerance towards all nations, but also of respect for their religions?

A certain gentleman,[39] an enemy neither to reason, nor to literature, nor to probity, nor to patriotism, was heard a little while ago to justify St Bar-

---

[39] Voltaire here refers to l'abbé Malvaux, whose *Accord de la religion et de l'humanité sur l'intolérance* (1762) he discusses at length below, ch. 24.

tholomew by comparing that massacre with the war of the Phocians, known as 'the holy war' as if it had been waged in support of dogma or to defend theological niceties. It had not. The purpose of the war was to determine the ownership of a certain field. Such is the point of all wars. Blades of corn are not articles of faith; no Greek city ever went to war over an opinion; and what, after all, does this gentle and modest man propose? Would he have us indulge in another holy war?

8

On whether the Romans were tolerant

In ancient Rome, from Romulus right up to the time when Christians disputed with Latin clerics, you will not find a single instance of a man persecuted for his religious convictions. Cicero was a sceptic about everything and Lucretius denied everything, yet neither of them was subjected to the mildest reproof. Intellectual licence was carried even further, as when the natural philosopher Pliny began his book with the statement that there was no God, or, if there were, it was the Sun. Speaking of the concept of Hell, Cicero said: *Non est anus tam excors quae credat* – 'there is no old fool so stupid as to believe in it'. And Juvenal wrote (Satire II, 152): *Nec pueri credunt* – 'children don't believe a word of it'. On the Roman stage they used to chant: *Post mortem nihil est, ipsaque mors nihil* – 'after death there is nothing, and death itself is nothing' (Seneca, *Troades*, chorus at the end of Act II).

Yes, we should abhor these notions. We can but forgive their appearance among a people whom the gospels had not yet enlightened. They are false, they are blasphemous, but we are bound to conclude that the Romans were uncommonly tolerant, for none of these opinions caused the slightest excitement.

The over-riding principle of the Roman senate and people in this regard was: *Deorum offensae deis curae* – 'if the gods are offended, it is a matter for the gods alone'. This sovereign people thought only of conquest, government, and how to civilise the universe. They were our law-givers as well as our conquerors. Caesar gave us slavery, laws and games, but not once did he attempt to force us to abandon our Druids, despite his being the supreme authority of a conquering nation.

The Romans did not follow all religions, nor did they bestow official recognition upon all of them, but they did permit them all to flourish. Under Numa,[40] they had no material object of worship, no images or statues. Soon, however, they erected some to those gods *majorum gentium* whom the Greeks had introduced. The law of the dozen tables, *Deos peregrinos ne colunto*, boils down to the precept that public recognition should only be given to the superior gods, those approved by the senate. There was a temple to Isis in Rome, until Tiberius demolished it when its priests, bribed by Mundus, arranged for this latter, under the name of the god Anubis, to sleep in the temple with a young woman called Paulina. It is true that we only have Josephus' account of this story, which is not contemporary; moreover, he was both credulous and given to embellishment. It is difficult to believe that, in the sophisticated reign of Tiberius, a lady of the highest rank could be quite such an imbecile as to imagine she was being pleasured by the god Anubis.[41]

Whether this anecdote be true or false, it remains a fact that an Egyptian cult was able to erect a temple in Rome with public consent. The Jews ran their businesses as early as the Punic wars, and there existed synagogues in Rome from the time of Augustus. These were preserved almost without interruption, just as they are still in modern Rome. Is there any better evidence that tolerance was considered by the Romans to be the most sacred of human rights?

We are told that as soon as the Christians appeared, they were persecuted by these very same Romans who never persecuted anyone. It seems to me that this story is demonstrably untrue, and I need no better witness than St Paul himself. In the Acts of the Apostles[42] we learn that when Paul was accused by the Jews of wishing to destroy Mosaic law and supplant it with Jesus Christ, James suggested that he have his head shaved and that he should seek purification in the temple with four Jews, *in order that the world should know that what they say of us is false and that you continue to observe the law of Moses.*

Whereupon, Paul the Christian proceeded to follow all the Jewish ceremonies for a period of seven days. The seven days were not yet exhausted, before the Jews of Asia recognised him and, noticing that he had entered the temple not only in the company of Jews but sometimes with gentiles as well, they screamed profanation. Paul was arrested, taken before the governor Felix, and finally brought to the attention of the tribunal of Festus. A throng of Jews demanded

[40] An early King of Rome, who ruled seven centuries before Christ, legendary for his love of peace and justice.
[41] Paulina, wife of a certain Saturninus, was a Roman noblewoman dedicated to the cult of Isis. Decius Mundus was in love with her, but she rejected him. With the help of priests who were only too willing to assist in his nefarious designs, he tried to win her over by claiming to be Anubis, a deity within this cult who had the body of a man and the head of a jackal, and he appears to have succeeded. Being rather vain, Mundus could not resist telling Paulina how he had tricked her, whereupon she urged her husband to ask the Emperor to have Mundus and his accomplices punished.
[42] Chapters 21, 24. [Voltaire's note]

his death, to which Festus made this reply: *It is not the custom in Rome to condemn a man before he has faced his accusers and had the opportunity to defend himself.*[43]

These words are all the more remarkable in that the Roman magistrate appears to have been moved by no consideration whatever for St Paul, whom he personally regarded with scorn. Deceived by the false light of his own reason, he took Paul for a lunatic, telling him to his face that he was possessed by madness, *multae te litterae ad insaniam convertunt.*[44] In offering his protection to a stranger for whom he could muster no respect, Festus demonstrated the basic fairness of Roman law.

Thus does Holy Scripture itself aver that the Romans were just, that they were not persecutors by any measure. It was not they who rose up against St Paul, but the Jews. James, the brother of Jesus, was stoned to death on the orders of a Sadducean Jew, not a Roman. The Jews stoned St Stephen all by themselves,[45] and when St Paul guarded the cloaks of the executioners, he was certainly not acting as a Roman citizen would.

The first Christians had no reason to quarrel with the Romans; their only enemies were the Jews, from whom they had begun to separate themselves. We are familiar with the implacable hatred borne by all members of a sect towards those who desert it. Without doubt, there were many riots in the synagogues of Rome. Suetonius says, in his *Life of Claudius: Judaeos, impulsore Christo assidue tumultuantes, Roma expulit.*[46] He was mistaken in assuming these tumults to have been at the instigation of Christ; he could not, after all, be expected to be well informed on the details of a race as despised in Rome as were the Jews. But he was not mistaken in his understanding of the reason for these mighty disputes. Suetonius was writing in the reign of Hadrian, in the second century AD. At that time the Romans did not distinguish Jew from Christian. This passage from Suetonius makes clear that the Romans, far from persecuting the early Christians, tried to control the Jews who oppressed them. They wished the Roman synagogues to evince the same tolerance towards their dissenting brothers as the senate allowed the synagogues. Moreover, the expelled Jews returned soon

---

43 Acts of the Apostles, 25:16. To be precise, Porcius Festus succeeded Felix as governor, and thereby inherited the prisoner Paul whom Felix had placed in custody. [Voltaire's note]

44 Acts, 26:24. [Voltaire's note] In the New English Bible, the passage reads, 'While Paul was thus making his defence, Festus shouted at the top of his voice, "Paul, you are raving; too much study is driving you mad."'

45 Although the Jews had lost the privilege of sitting in judgement and executing criminals, ever since the banishment of Archelaus and the establishment of Roman government in Judea as a province of the Empire, nevertheless the Romans had turned a blind eye when the Jews acted zealously, such as when they stoned to death one of their own people whom they thought guilty of blasphemy. [Voltaire's note]

46 The passage in Suetonius' *The Twelve Caesars*, in the translation by Robert Graves, reads 'Because the Jews at Rome caused continuous disturbances at the instigation of Chrestus [i.e. Christ], he expelled them from the city.'

afterwards; they even received honours and position, despite laws which supposedly excluded them from any such: we have this from both Dion Cassius[47]
and Ulpian.[48] Is it possible that after the destruction of Jerusalem the Roman
emperors would have showered honours upon the Jews, and at the same time
persecuted Christians, butchered them and thrown them to the lions, when they
regarded Christians as a sect of the Jews?

We are told that Nero persecuted them. Tacitus informs us that they were
charged with the burning of Rome and abandoned to the fury of the people. Was
it their faith which caused this accusation to be made? Surely not. We might as
well say that the Chinese whom the Dutch slaughtered, a few years since, in the
suburbs of Batavia, were sacrificed on the altar of religion![49] However great the
need we may have to deceive ourselves, it is quite impossible for us to attribute
to intolerance the disaster which, under Nero, befell a few unhappy half-Jews
and half-Christians.

[47] Dion Cassius, an historian born about AD 155, wrote a history of Rome, in Greek.
[48] Ulpianus, *Digest.*, 1, ii. 'Eis qui judaicam superstitionem sequuntur honores adipisci permiserunt, etc.' [Voltaire's note] Ulpian (Domitius Ulpianus) was one of the most senior and respected jurists of Rome in the early third century. But he was regarded as an enemy by the soldiers, who sought every excuse to vilify him. A three-day riot between the people and the military, with the former attempting to defend Ulpian, ended with his murder by a mob of soldiers, almost at the feet of the Emperor.
[49] Batavia, a city on the north coast of Java, was capital of all the Dutch settlements in the Far East. Of the various peoples who lived there, the Chinese were the most grotesquely oppressed by the occupiers. Voltaire here refers to the Dutch massacre of twelve thousand Chinese in 1740.

9
On martyrs

After this came the Christian martyrs. It is extremely difficult to determine exactly why these martyrs were condemned to death. Nevertheless, I venture to suggest that under the first Caesars not one of them was executed merely on account of his religion, for all religions were allowed. Otherwise, we would have to believe that the authorities rooted out and persecuted a handful of obscure adherents to a particular sect at a time when absolutely all the other sects were tolerated.

The emperors Titus, Trajan, Antoninus, Decius, these were no barbarians. Are we to imagine that they would deprive the Christians alone of a liberty enjoyed by the whole empire? Might they even have been accused of harbouring some mysterious secrets, when the mysteries of Isis, of Mithras, of the goddess of Assyria, all foreign to the predominant Roman cult, were permitted free rein? No, it is clear that their persecution issued from other causes, and that precise and especial hatreds, supported by political motivation, were responsible for spilling the blood of the Christians.

When, for example, St Lawrence refused to surrender to the Prefect of Rome, Cornelius Secularius, Christian money which he held in safe-keeping, it was only to be expected that the Prefect and the Emperor should be put out. They were not to know that St Lawrence had distributed this money to the poor, that he had in fact done a charitable and holy act. They considered him a rebel, and put him to death.[50]

---

[50] According to tradition, Lawrence, one of the seven deacons of Rome, was ordered by the prefect Cornelius Secularius to hand over the valuables of the Church, whereupon he assembled the poor and the sick and presented them to the prefect with the words 'Here is the Church's treasure.' He is said to have been martyred by being roasted alive on a grid. It is more likely, however, that he was beheaded, as Pope Sixtus had been four days earlier. This martyrdom occurred in 258.

Let us now look at the martyrdom of St Polyeuctes.[51] Was he killed only because of his religion? He makes his way into the temple where sacrifices are offered to the gods for the victory of the Emperor Decius;[52] he insults the priests, overturns the altars, shatters the statues; is there a country in the world which would forgive such an outrage? The Christian who publicly tore up a decree of the Emperor Diocletian,[53] thereby bringing upon the heads of his co-religionists the terrible persecution which disfigured the last two years of this prince's reign, was not zealous according to proper definition. Yet he had the misfortune to be responsible for the disaster which ensued. This kind of rash religious enthusiasm which exploded from time to time and was even denounced by several fathers of the Church, is most probably the root cause of all those persecutions.

I do not, of course, intend any comparison between the first Sacramentarians and the Early Christians, or to give equal weight to Error and Truth. Nevertheless, Farel,[54] the predecessor of Jean Calvin, did precisely the same at Arles as Polyeuctes did in Armenia. A statue of St Antony the Hermit[55] was being carried through the streets in procession. Farel and some of his friends fell upon the monks who were carrying St Antony, beat them, chased them off, and threw St Antony in the river. Farel escaped the death he deserved because he had time to take flight. Had he been content to tell the monks that he did not believe a crow had taken half a loaf to St Antony the Hermit in its beak, nor that St Antony had been in conversation with centaurs and satyrs, he would have deserved a strong reprimand for having disturbed the peace; if, on the other hand, he had gone from the procession and quietly contemplated the story of the crow, the centaurs and the satyrs, and kept his thoughts to himself, there would have been nothing to reproach him with.

Could the Romans have suffered the unspeakable Antinous[56] to be placed in the ranks of their secondary gods, and at the same time have torn to pieces and thrown to the lions men whose only fault was to have peacefully worshipped a true one? Could they conceivably have recognised a supreme and sovereign

[51] According to legend, Polyeuctes, a Roman centurion, was supposed to have been martyred in 250, but there is no reason to think he ever existed.

[52] The Emperor Decius reigned from 249 to 251, and died in a battle with the Goths; his body was never found.

[53] The Emperor Diocletian (284–305) was an active persecutor of Christians, the independence of whose church he regarded as a challenge to his authority.

[54] Guillaume Farel (1489–1565), a French reformer noted for the passion and grimness of his oratory, friend and supporter of Calvin.

[55] St Antony the Hermit, born near Memphis, Egypt, in 251, was known as the father of monasticism.

[56] Antinous was a youth from Claudiopolis in Bithynia, famed for his beauty. He became the favourite of the Emperor Hadrian until he drowned himself in the Nile. Hadrian then named cities after him, caused medals to be struck in his memory, and raised him to the rank of the gods. Temples were even built for his worship.

God,[57] superior to all the secondary gods, as is attested in their formula *Deus optimus maximus*, and at the same time have pursued men who worshipped only one God?

It is simply not believable that Roman emperors ever subjected the Christians to an Inquisition, by which is meant that people were sent to interrogate them about matters of faith. They did not bother Jew, Syrian, Egyptian, Druid, poet or philosopher on this score. The martyrs, therefore, were people who rose up in anger against false gods. No doubt they were correct in refusing to believe in these gods, and pious to a degree. But in the end one is bound to conclude that, if they were not content to worship God in spirit and in truth, but needed to make violent protest against the established religion, however absurd it might be, then it is they who were intolerant.

Tertullian,[58] in his *Apology*, confirms that Christians were regarded as radicals. The term is doubtless unfair, but it does indicate that it was not by virtue of their religion that Christians provoked the attention of the magistrates. Tertullian further acknowledges that, when there were public celebrations to mark the emperors' military victories, Christians refused to decorate their doors with laurel branches in their honour; it is not difficult to see how this mischievous affectation might be construed as a treasonable offence.[59]

The first time the might of Roman law was directed against the Christians was under Domitian, and then it was limited to a banishment which lasted less than

---

[57] We need only turn to Virgil to be convinced that the Romans worshipped one supreme God, the Sovereign of all celestial beings.

> ...O! qui res hominum deumque
> Aeternis regis imperiis, et fulmine terres. (Aen., 1, 233–4)
> O pater, o hominum divumque aeterna potestas, etc. (Aen., x, 18)

And Horace expresses himself in even stronger terms:

> Unde nil majus generatur ipso,
> Nec viget quidquam simile, aut secundum. (Bk 1, ode xii, 17–18)

In those mysteries into which almost all Romans were initiated, only the unity of God was spoken of. Witness the fine hymn of Orpheus; and read the letter from Maximus to St Augustine, in which he says that 'none but fools can deny the existence of a Supreme Being'. Longinus, who was a pagan, writes to St Augustine that 'there is but one God, who is incomprehensible and ineffable'. Lactantius, who certainly cannot be charged with being too indulgent, admits in his fifth book that 'the Romans subjected all the other deities to the one Supreme God'. Tertullian also acknowledges in his *Apology* (ch. xxiv) that the whole Roman Empire recognised a single God, ruler of the world, whose power and majesty are infinite. Again, look at Plato, Cicero's master in philosophy, and you will see that he taught that there is only one God, whom we ought to love and adore, and endeavour to resemble in justice and holiness. Epictetus in his dungeon and Mark Anthony on his throne say the same thing in a hundred different places. [Voltaire's note]

[58] Quintus Septimus Florens Tertullianus (*c.* 155–*c.* 222), a convert to Christianity, is the earliest name in Christian Latin literature, an apologist of great authority.

[59] *Apologeticum*, chs. 39, 35. [Voltaire's note]

one year: *facile coeptum repressit, restitutis etiam quos relegaverat*, says Tertullian (Ch. 5). Lactantius,[60] whose florid style sometimes gets the better of him, agrees that from Domitian to Decius the Church was tranquil and flourishing. This long period of peace was eventually interrupted, he says, when that 'execrable animal' Decius oppressed the Christian faith: *exstitit enim post annos plurimos exsecrable animal Decius qui vexaret Ecclesiam (Apologeticum*, Ch. 4).[61]

I do not intend to discuss here the opinion advanced by the scholarly Mr Dodwell[62] concerning the small number of true martyrs; but if the Romans had persecuted the Christian religion, and if the senate had put so many poor innocents to a cruel and unprecedented death, if they had plunged Christians into boiling oil and abandoned totally naked virgins to lions in the Colosseum, why then did they leave all the earliest bishops of Rome in peace? St Irenaeus[63] can find only one of these bishops to count among the martyrs, namely Telesphorus in the year AD 139, and there is no proof whatever that he was put to death.[64] Zephirinus governed the flock in Rome for eighteen years and died in his sleep in the year 219. It is true that ancient lists of martyrs include nearly all the first Popes, but that is because the word 'martyr' was then only used in its proper sense of 'witness'; it did not signify being put to death.

It is difficult to reconcile this passion for persecution with the freedom which the Christians enjoyed to assemble fifty-six councils, which ecclesiastical writers inform us took place during the first three centuries.

Certainly there were some persecutions; but had they been as violent as we are told, it is more than probable that Tertullian, who wrote so powerfully against the established religion, would not have died in his bed. Of course the emperors did not read his *Apology*; an obscure tract composed in Africa was unlikely to come to the attention of men charged with the governance of the world. But it must have been known to those who moved within the circle of the proconsul of Africa, it must have excited much hatred against its author, and yet he did not suffer martyrdom.

[60] Lactantius Firmianus (*c.* 260–*c.* 340), the 'Christian Cicero', was a native of North Africa who taught rhetoric at Nicomedia and was the most eloquent Christian apologist of his time.

[61] The edict of the Emperor Decius (249–51), intentionally or not, unleashed a wave of persecutions in 250. Decius had murdered his predecessor Philip, who had been reputedly 'soft' on Christians, and presumably to strengthen his legitimacy as well as enthuse the people with a 'cause', he issued an edict which ordered sacrifice to the gods throughout the empire. He did not ask for sacrifice to himself, or the empire, and did not specify which gods, leaving the locals to choose their own favourite deity. Of course there was only one group which would not recognise any god but their own, and that was the Christians, so it was they who were conspicuously punished for disregarding the edict.

[62] Henry Dodwell the younger (d. 1784), author of *Christianity not founded on Argument* (1742).

[63] Irenaeus, one of the most important theologians of the second century, Bishop of Lyons and writer.

[64] Telesphorus, Pope and martyr, Greek by birth, was the seventh successor to Peter. He is traditionally supposed to have been martyred under the Emperor Hadrian and his body buried in the Vatican, but modern excavations can find no trace of him.

Origen[65] taught the Christian faith openly in Alexandria, and was not put to death for it. This same Origen, who spoke so frankly to both pagans and Christians, who proclaimed Jesus to the former and denied the Trinity to the latter, openly admits in his third book against Celsus[66] that 'there have been very few martyrs, and even they have been separated by long intervals; and yet the Christians neglect no opportunity to propagate their religion throughout the world, preaching in every city, town and village'.

It is certain that priests of other religions might easily have suspected these ceaseless journeys of having seditious intent, and yet the missionaries were tolerated even by the ever turbulent, cowardly and fractious Egyptian people, who were capable of tearing a Roman to pieces for having killed a cat; the Egyptians have at all times and in all ages been contemptible, whatever admirers of the Pyramids may say to the contrary.

Who is there more likely to have incurred the wrath of both spiritual and secular authority than St Gregory Thaumaturgus,[67] the disciple of Origen? Gregory had been visited during the night by a vision, namely an old man sent to him by God and accompanied by a woman bathed in light; the woman was the Virgin Mary and the old man was St John the Evangelist. St John dictated to him a message which he then set out to preach everywhere. In Neocaesarea he was obliged by inclement weather to spend the night in a temple infested with oracles. He made the sign of the cross several times, and the next morning the high priest was astonished to discover that the demons who normally responded to his call had suddenly fallen silent and would reveal nothing. He summoned them again. The devils came only to announce that they would never return. They informed him that they could reside no more in the temple, for Gregory had spent the night there and made the sign of the cross.

Upon which, the high priest seized hold of Gregory, who boldly told him, 'I may expel demons from where I like, and equally introduce them where it may please me. In that case', said the priest, 'bring them back to my temple.' So Gregory tore a piece of paper from the book he carried in his hand, and wrote

---

[65] Origen was the son of Christian parents, born possibly in Alexandria and probably in the year 185. His commentaries on the Scriptures, and his huge output of books on various aspects of Christian philosophy and spiritual analysis, make him virtually the father of Christian dogma, the first and most influential of the great teachers.

[66] Celsus was a pagan philosopher of the second century, whose thesis against the Christian faith was published and refuted by Origen in a line-by-line argument.

[67] Gregory, Bishop of Neocaesarea, was born in the province of Pontus of pagan parents and received a good education in law and literature. At the age of twenty, he went with his brother to Palestine where they studied for five years with Origen, whose influence on Gregory was profound. Both brothers were converted to Christianity by Origen and baptised, Gregory returning to Neocaesarea as a missionary and, very soon afterwards, bishop. He is said to have converted virtually the entire population of Neocaesarea in the course of the next thirty years.

upon it these words: *Gregory to Satan, I command thee to come once more into this temple*. The scrap of paper was placed on the altar. The demons obeyed, and rendered their oracles that day as they had done before, after which Gregory banished them anew and they were never heard of again.

These facts in the life of St Gregory Thaumaturgus we owe to St Gregory of Nyssa.[68] The pagan priests most surely would have had cause to be angry with Gregory and, in their ignorance, to send him before the magistrates. And yet they did nothing of the sort, and this man, their most mortal enemy, was not made to suffer persecution of any kind.

It is said that St Cyprian[69] was the first Bishop of Carthage to be condemned to death. The martyrdom of St Cyprian took place in the year 258 of our era; it follows from this that for a very long period no Bishop of Carthage had ever been murdered on account of his religion. History does not relate what calumnies were hurled at Cyprian, who were his enemies, or why the Proconsul of Africa found him irksome. St Cyprian wrote to Cornelius, the Bishop of Rome: 'There has recently been some popular feeling against me in Carthage, and twice it has been bruited I should be thrown to the lions.' It is indeed probable that the extravagant emotions of those fierce Carthaginians were responsible for Cyprian's death, and it is equally certain that the Emperor Gallus did not sentence him to death from afar for his religious views, since he suffered Cornelius,[70] with similar views, to live under his very nose.

There may be so many hidden causes underlying the apparent cause, so many submerged springs which, combined, lead to the persecution of a man, that it is impossible centuries later to disentangle the unavowed motives for the misery of the most famous, still less to identify why a particular individual, known only to his own group of intimates, should have suffered the ultimate ordeal.

Note that St Gregory Thaumaturgus and St Dionysius, the Bishop of Alexandria,[71] were contemporary with St Cyprian and were not martyred. How is it that, when they were at least as well known as this Bishop of Carthage, if not more so, they were left in peace? Why should St Cyprian be put to death rather than they? Does it not seem likely that the one fell victim to personal and

---

[68] Gregory of Nyssa (335–95) was a younger brother of St Basil the Great. Born in the province of Cappadocia, adjacent to Pontus, he became a noted theologian and apologist.

[69] Cyprian (200–58) began his working life as a barrister, but converted to Christianity at the age of forty-six. Two years later he was made Bishop of Carthage. He was one of the first victims of a new wave of persecution brought by the Emperor Valerian in 258. Refusing to sacrifice to Roman gods, he was sentenced to death. The execution took place before a vast crowd, many of whom threw their garments at him in the hope they would be stained with his blood.

[70] Cornelius, 'Pope and martyr,' was born in Rome and died in exile in Civitavecchia in 253. There is no evidence that he was martyred.

[71] Dionysius of Alexandria was a pupil of Origen, whom he succeeded as director of the catechetical school for fourteen years. He was made Bishop of Alexandria in 247, and three years later was arrested and exiled. He eventually returned to Alexandria in 261.

powerful enemies, to slander informed by political motives so often masquerading as religion, while the others were fortunate enough not to come up against the wickedness of man?

It is scarcely possible that St Ignatius[72] should have suffered death, in the reign of the compassionate and just Emperor Trajan,[73] merely for being a Christian, since other Christians were allowed to accompany him and console him when he was taken to Rome. There had been frequent uprisings in the turbulent city of Antioch, where Ignatius was an undercover bishop to the Christian community; it is perfectly possible that innocent Christians were wrongly and maliciously blamed for this seditious activity, thus attracting the attention of the government which found itself, not for the first time, deceived.

St Simeon,[74] for example, was accused before Shapur of spying for the Romans. According to the account of his martyrdom, King Shapur is alleged to have invited him to worship the sun. But it is well known that the Persians did not worship the sun; they considered it to be a symbol and manifestation of the Ultimate and Original Good, the Oromases or Oromasdes; in other words they acknowledged God the Creator.

However forgiving one may be, it is impossible to resist some feeling of indignation against those glib phrase-mongers who accuse Diocletian of having persecuted Christians from the day he ascended his throne. Let us call as witness Eusebius of Caesarea;[75] his testimony cannot be impugned when the favourite of Constantine and his eulogist, a man passionately hostile to all the preceding emperors, suddenly finds cause to praise their actions, then he must earn our respectful attention. This is what he says: 'For a long time the emperors treated the Christians with many displays of goodwill. They entrusted provinces to them, allowed many to live in the palace, they even married Christian girls. Diocletian took as his wife Prisca, whose daughter married Maximianus Galerius', and so it goes on.[76]

We should learn from this decisive testimony to desist from facile calumny; and we should wonder whether the persecution instigated by Galerius, after

---

[72] Ignatius of Antioch is the author of seven letters to Church leaders, which offer rare witness of Christian values and practices less than a century after Christ's death. He was made Bishop of Antioch, where he was arrested and sentenced to death in 107. He was then taken to Rome to be thrown among wild beasts and torn apart in the amphitheatre (nowadays called the Colosseum).

[73] Trajan (98–117) did much to protect Christians against the Jews, ruling that they had the right to a proper trial before their accusers and that judges should not heed slander from concealed or anonymous sources. His successor Hadrian (117–38) confirmed the ruling.

[74] Simeon Barsabba'e, chief bishop of the Christians in Persia, bore the brunt of the cruel persecutions sanctioned by King Shapur II, who resisted Constantine's desire to make the empire Christian. St Simeon refused to conform to the Persian religion, and was put to death at Ctesiphon in 341 (some say in April 344).

[75] Eusebius was born in Caesarea about 260, studied under Pamphilus (a pupil of Origen's), and became Bishop of Caesarea and one of the most prolific authors among the early Christian writers.

[76] *Historia Ecclesiastica*, bk VIII. [Voltaire's note]

nineteen years of beneficent and mild rule, might not be due to some political intrigue about which we know nothing.

We should acknowledge the absurdity of that fable of the legion of Thebans or Thebeans, massacred, we have been told, solely because of their religion. It is ridiculous to suggest the legion was dragged all the way from Asia through the St Bernard Pass.[77] It is simply not possible that they should be summoned from Asia to suppress an uprising amongst the Gauls, one whole year after that uprising had already been subdued. It is no more possible that six thousand infantry and seven hundred cavalry should have been slaughtered in a pass where two hundred men could easily halt an entire army. The narrative of this so-called butchery begins with an obvious invention: 'When the earth groaned beneath the tyranny of Diocletian, the sky was thronged with martyrs.' Now, the story as it unfolds relates to the year 286, at the very time when Diocletian most favoured the Christians and the Roman Empire was at its most relaxed. Finally, the one fact which ought to put a stop to all debate is this: there never was a Theban legion. The Romans were too proud and too intelligent to have established a legion composed of those Egyptians who were of use to them only as slaves, *Verna Canopi*; they might just as well have founded a Jewish legion! We have the names of the thirty-two legions which provided the principal forces of the Roman Empire, and there is no mention of a Theban legion. This is a tale which belongs with those acrostic verses wherein the Sibyls purported to predict the miracles of Jesus Christ, or with many other alleged adventures with which prolific zealotry seduces the credulous.

[77] According to legend, the 'Theban legion' was composed of Christian soldiers from Egypt under the command of St Maurice. Refusing to sacrifice to heathen gods, they were slaughtered to a man on the order of the Romans. The story is told by St Eucherius of Lyon, writing in 444, about 160 years after the event, and it is possible that a small unit of soldiers was put to death and their martyrdom subsequently elevated them to a legion and swelled their numbers. The abbey of St Maurice stands on the presumed site of the massacre at Agaune in Switzerland. The St Bernard Pass, of course, was not then so named, Bernard being a tenth-century figure.

10
On the dangers of false legends and persecution

Falsehood has for too long held sway over the minds of men. It is time we sought to discover the few truths which we may discern through the vast clouds of fable which cover Roman history from the time of Tacitus and Suetonius, and which have nearly always smothered the annals of other nations in the ancient world.

How on earth are we to believe, for example, that the Romans, a serious, austere people from whom we have inherited our system of law, should have condemned Christian virgins from respectable families to a life of prostitution? Anyone who suggests such a thing does not know the grave dignity of those legislators nor the severity with which they punished the transgressions of the Vestals. It is the *Actes sincères* of Ruinart[78] which relate these squalid tales; but one may ask, should we lend as much credence to the *Actes* of Ruinart as to the Acts of the Apostles? These *Actes sincères*, according to Bollandus,[79] say that in the city of Ancyra[80] there were seven Christian virgins, each one about seventy years old, who were sentenced by the governor Theodectus to give their bodies to every young man of the city; when nobody availed himself of the offer, which was hardly surprising, the governor made them serve naked at the mysteries of Diana, which, as we know, could only be witnessed from behind a veil! St Theodotus, who was in fact an inn-keeper, but no less an enthusiast for that,

[78] Dom Thierry Ruinart (1657–1709), *Acta primorum martyrum sincera*, Paris, 1689. The book went into several editions, and his correspondence is preserved in the Bibliothèque Nationale, Paris.
[79] John Bolland, Jesuit father after whom the order of Bollandists in Belgium is named. He inherited an ambitious publishing concept from Heribert Rosweyde, who planned an anthology of the lives and legends of the saints, arranged according to the calendar, by days. When he died in 1629 he had collected a large amount of material but had not yet started work. Bolland carried the work forward to astonishing fruition. The *Acta Sanctorum* eventually spread to sixty-three volumes, published over a period of two hundred and sixty years.
[80] The ancient city of Galatia, in Asia Minor.

ardently beseeched God to grant death to these holy spinsters, lest they should succumb to temptation. God answered his prayer. The governor had them thrown into a lake with stones around their necks. Straight afterwards they appeared before St Theodotus and begged him 'not to allow their bodies to be eaten by fish'; those were their actual words.

In the middle of the night, the holy publican and his mates went to the edge of the lake, which was guarded by soldiers. They were preceded by a heavenly torch to show them the way. When they arrived at the point where the guards were stationed, a celestial horseman, armed to the teeth, chased the soldiers off with his sword. St Theodotus recovered the virgins' bodies from the lake; as a result of which he was brought before the governor, and the celestial horseman failed to intervene to prevent his head being severed from his body. While we shall not cease to maintain that we venerate true martyrs, at the same time we must admit that this story of Bollandus and Ruinart does present some difficulties.

Do we need to repeat here the story of the young St Romanus? He was thrown to the fire, says Eusebius, and the Jews who saw what happened began insulting Jesus Christ for allowing His followers to be burnt alive, whereas God had rescued Shadrach, Meshach and Abednego from the fiery furnace.[81] The Jews had scarcely finished talking when St Romanus walked triumphant from the flames. The Emperor ordered him to be pardoned and told the judge he did not want to get entangled with God in any way – strange words indeed for Diocletian to utter! The judge, in contravention of the Emperor's clemency, gave orders for St Romanus' tongue to be cut out, and though he had executioners aplenty, chose a doctor to perform the operation. Young Romanus, a stammerer since birth, started talking volubly as soon as his tongue was removed. The doctor was thereupon reprimanded, and to demonstrate that he had conducted the amputation according to the rules of his art, selected a passer-by and cut out the poor man's tongue in exactly the same way, as a result of which he dropped dead on the spot; 'for', adds the learned author, 'anatomy teaches us that a man without a tongue cannot live for long'. If Eusebius really did write such twaddle and it was not added by subsequent scribes, how could we view any part of his History with confidence?

We are given the martyrdom of St Felicity and her seven children, sent to their death by the wise and pious Antoninus; or so we are told, for the author of this narrative remains anonymous.[82]

It is very likely that some scribbler more noted for enthusiasm than accuracy

---

[81] Daniel, 3.

[82] Traditionally, Felicity and her seven sons, all Christians, refused to sacrifice to the gods and were sentenced to die in different ways, the mother last of all. This legend could be adapted, as Voltaire suggests, from an Old Testament story of a Jewish mother and her seven faithful sons (2 Maccabees, 7).

wanted to copy the story of the Maccabees. This is how it begins: 'St Felicity was a Roman woman who lived during the reign of Antoninus.' From these words it is clear the author was not a contemporary. He says that the Praetor passed judgement on her at his court at the Campus Martius; but the Prefect of Rome held his court at the Capitol and not on the Campus Martius, which, having once served as place for a *comitia*,[83] was at that time used for military parades, chariot races and other competitive games. This mistake alone illustrates the unreliability of the author.

It is further stated that after judgement had been passed, the Emperor assigned to other judges the task of seeing that sentence was duly executed, a proceeding entirely at variance with the formalities which then obtained, and which have moreover operated in all ages.

There is even a St Hippolytus, supposedly dragged to his death by a team of horses, as was Hippolytus the son of Theseus. But this punishment was unknown in ancient Rome, and the mere coincidence of the name has given birth to this fable.[84]

Note also that in the narratives of martyrdom, composed by Christians and by no one else, there is nearly always a multitude of Christians who go freely into the prison, who accompany the martyr to his death, who collect his blood, bury his body, and perform miracles with his relics. Had the sole object of persecution been religion, then why did the authorities not murder these self-professed Christians, who openly gave succour to condemned men and who were accused of casting spells with the remains of the martyrs' bodies? Surely they would have been treated as we have treated the Vaudois,[85] the Albigensians,[86] the Hussites,[87] the various sects of Protestants. We have slaughtered them and burnt them alive without distinction of age or sex. Among the well-attested cases of persecution in ancient times, is there one which, in character, comes anywhere near the terror of St Bartholomew or the Irish massacres? Is there anything like that annual festival held in Toulouse, a truly wicked festival which ought to be abolished for all time, in which an entire population marches in procession to thank God and congratulate one another for having massacred, two hundred years ago, four thousand of the city's inhabitants?

[83] The *comitia* was an assembly which passed legislation, heard appeals, and was responsible for the election of consuls and praetors.

[84] There was indeed a St Hippolytus, a priest and writer who lived from 170 to 235, and was exiled to Sardinia with Pope Pontianus. The other Hippolytus to whom Voltaire here makes scornful reference was a Christian invention, by analogy with Hippolytus, son of Theseus.

[85] Inhabitants of the canton of Vaud, in Switzerland, which became entirely Protestant thanks to the oratory of Farel.

[86] Albigenses or Albigensians is the name given to the reformers in the south of France in the twelfth century, who were centred more on Toulouse than Albi, and are sometimes mentioned synonymously with Huguenots. They publicly deplored the corruption of the clergy.

[87] Followers of the Czech reformer John Hus (1369–1415), who was much influenced by Wycliffe.

I say it with repugnance, but with truth: it is we, we Christians, who have been the persecutors, the executioners, the assassins! And of whom? Of our own brothers. It is we who have laid waste a hundred cities, with the Bible or the crucifix in our hands, we who have spilt blood and ignited faggots with scarcely a pause from the reign of Constantine up to the insane cannibalism of the Cévennes,[88] a wickedness which is now, thank Heaven, at an end.

We still sometimes send to the gallows some poor wretches from Poitou, Vivarais, Valence or Montauban. Since 1745 we have hanged eight of those people called Evangelists or lay preachers, whose only crime has been to pray God for the King in *patois* and to give a drop of wine and a scrap of leavened bread to a few simple-minded peasants. None of this is known in Paris, where people live only for pleasure and rest in complacent ignorance of everything that happens in the provinces or abroad. These trials are despatched in under an hour, faster than is required to pass judgement on a deserter. If the King were properly informed, he would use his prerogative to bestow royal pardon.

In no Protestant country are Catholic priests treated in this way. There are more than a hundred in England and Ireland; they are known to the authorities, and they were entirely unmolested throughout the last war.

Are we French destined always to be the last to adopt the civilised ways of other nations? They have put their houses in order; when are we going to bring order to our own? It took us sixty years to accept the demonstrations of Newton; we have barely started to have the courage to save the lives of our children through inoculation; only very recently have we begun to adopt correct agricultural principles; when shall we adopt equally correct principles of humanity? And on what grounds may we loftily reproach the pagans for having created martyrs, when we have been guilty of similar cruelties in similar circumstances?

Supposing we grant that the Romans put to death a multitude of Christians solely on account of their religion; in which case the Romans were utterly to be condemned. Should we then wish to emulate them by committing like injustices? And when we reprove them for having been intolerant, should we then strive to be intolerant ourselves?

If there be somebody sufficiently devoid of good faith, or sufficiently fanatical, to tell me now: Why do you come to expose our mistakes and our deficiencies? Why destroy our spurious miracles and our fantastic legends? They nourish the piety of many; some errors are useful; you should not attempt to remove a

---

[88] The war of the Cévennes was one of the most bloodthirsty in the history of France. When the Edict of Nantes was revoked in 1685 and attempts were made to stamp out the Huguenots by torture and repression, the peasants of the Cévennes (sometimes known as *Camisards* because of the shirt they wore over their armour to distinguish friend from foe) organised themselves into guerrilla resistance, murdering Catholic clergy and submitting Catholic churches to wholesale destruction. The punishment visited upon them was vicious: four hundred and sixty villages were razed.

malignant growth if in so doing you risk the destruction of the body which harbours it. This is how I would reply:

'All these false miracles by which you unsettle the confidence due to true ones, and all these absurd legends with which you clutter the truth of the Gospels, stifle religion in the hearts of men. Too many people who would like to educate themselves, and lack the time to educate themselves properly, will say: The ministers of my religion have deceived me, therefore there is no truth in religion; better to depend upon the voice of Nature than that of Error; I prefer to entrust myself to natural laws than to the fictions of men. Yet others will have the misfortune to go even further; they will see that they have been misled and restrained by falsehood and, refusing the natural restraints of truth, logic brings them towards atheism; some therefore become intellectually depraved because others have been cynical and cruel.'

These are the inevitable consequences of pious fraud and superstition. Men generally only reason up to a certain point. It is a very bad argument to say, 'Voragine,[89] author of the *Golden Legend*, and the Jesuit Ribadeneira,[90] who compiled *Flower of the Saints*, have both told me a load of nonsense, therefore God does not exist: the Catholics have murdered a certain number of Huguenots, and the Huguenots have in their turn assassinated a goodly number of Catholics, therefore God does not exist: the confessional, the Holy Communion, and all the sacraments have been used to cloak the most hideous crimes, therefore God does not exist.' I would reach an entirely different conclusion: God does exist, and after this transient life of ours, in which we have misunderstood Him so disastrously and committed so many crimes in His name, He will comfort us in our distress at the memory of such catastrophes. For if we count the religious wars, the forty papal schisms, which have nearly all been bloody, the lies, which have nearly always brought calamity in their wake, the irreconcilable hatreds born of different opinions, and if we observe all the evil which results from false zeal, then we see that men have for long carried with them their own Hell on earth.

[89] Jacopo da Varazze (1230–98), known in French as Jacques de Voragine and in English as James of Voragine, an Italian priest and hagiographer who tried to restore peace between the Guelfs and the Ghibellines in Genoa, where he was made Archbishop in 1292.

[90] Pedro Ribadeneira (1527–1611) was born at Toledo and received by Ignatius Loyola into the Society of Jesus at the age of thirteen. He is best known as the first biographer of Loyola, but his *Flos Sanctorum*, which Voltaire here mocks, was a naive collection of saints' lives, dramatically superseded by the work of the Bollandists.

11
The consequences of intolerance

Is each individual citizen, then, to be permitted to believe only in what his reason tells him, to think only what his reason, be it enlightened or misguided, may dictate? Yes, indeed he should, provided always that he threatens no disturbance to public order.[91] For a man is under no obligation to believe or not to believe. His duties are to respect the laws and customs of his country, and if you claim that it is a crime not to believe in the prevailing religion, you are pointing the finger of accusation against our ancestors, the first Christians, and you are justifying the actions of those you previously blamed for putting them to death.

You will answer that there is the world of difference, that all the other religions are man-made and only the Roman Apostolic Church is the work of God. But in all conscience, does the fact that our religion is divinely inspired mean that it must rule through hatred, ferocity, banishment, confiscation, imprisonment, torture, murder, and the giving of thanks to God for murder? The more the Christian religion is divine, the less does it belong to man to control it; if God has made it, then God will sustain it without your help. You know that intolerance begets either hypocrites or rebels; what an appalling choice! Finally, would you wish to uphold by the power of the executioner the religion of a God who died at the hands of executioners and who preached only gentleness and patience?

Reflect, I implore you, on the truly dreadful consequences of intolerance sanctioned by law. If a citizen living in a society with a certain latitude and declining to profess the religion of that society could legally be stripped of his worldly goods, thrown into a dungeon, and murdered, what exceptional circum-

---

91 See Locke's excellent letter on tolerance. [Voltaire's note]

49

stances would exempt the first in the land from similar punishments? In religion the sovereign and the beggar are equals; it is a fact that more than fifty learned men and monks have affirmed the monstrous doctrine that it is lawful to depose, even to assassinate, monarchs who dare to think differently from the established Church; and the parliaments of this kingdom have repeatedly condemned such abominable decisions taken by abominable theologians.

The blood of Henri le Grand was scarcely cold when the Parliament of Paris issued a decree establishing the independence of the Crown as a fundamental law. Cardinal Duperron, who owed his promotion to Henri le Grand, spoke up against this decree in the assembly of 1614 and managed to have it suppressed. All the journals of the day report the words used by Duperron[92] in his harangue. 'If a prince were to declare himself Arian,'[93] he said, 'we should be obliged to depose him.'

No, my Lord Cardinal, we certainly should not. I might grant for a moment your whimsical proposition that one of our kings, having read the history of the synods and of the fathers of the Church, and having been struck by the words *my Father has greater power than I*,[94] and taking them perhaps too literally, might vacillate between the Council of Nicaea[95] and that of Constantinople[96] and finally declare himself in favour of Eusebius of Nicomedia; still, I should not the less be obedient to my King for that, I should not consider myself less bound by my oath of allegiance, and if you dared to rise in rebellion against him, and I were placed in judgement upon you, I would roundly pronounce you to be guilty of High Treason.

I have curtailed an argument which Duperron did indeed pursue further, but this is not the place to examine in depth such revolting fantasies. I shall limit myself to pointing out, along with every decent citizen, that one did not owe allegiance to Henri IV because he received the sacrament at Chartres, but because the incontestable right of birth placed upon his head a crown which he graced with his courage and goodness.

[92] Jacques Davy Duperron (1556–1618) abjured Protestantism and preached before the King. His funeral oration on Ronsard and his eulogy for Mary Queen of Scots induced him to take orders, and he subsequently instructed Henri IV in the Catholic religion. The King made him Bishop of Évreux, the Pope made him cardinal.

[93] Named after Arius, a fourth-century presbyter in Alexandria, who gave his name to the first and most dramatic schism in the Christian Church. The Arian doctrine denied that Christ was consubstantial with God, and held that his nature was human rather than divine and that he could not be considered as co-eternal with God the Father.

[94] John, 14:28.

[95] The Council of Nicaea (today Iznik, in Turkey) in the year 325 was the first ecumenical council, at which many of the doctrines of the Christian faith were formulated or confirmed, most significantly the doctrine of the Trinity, in opposition to the Arian heresy.

[96] The second ecumenical council took place in Constantinople in 381, and was attended by bishops from the eastern faith. The council reaffirmed the Nicene creed and condemned all opposing doctrines.

Let it be permitted therefore to say that, according to the same birthright, every citizen must be heir to the estate of his father and does not deserve to be deprived thereof, nor dragged to the gallows, on the grounds that he agrees with Ratramnus[97] against Radbertus Paschasius,[98] or with Berengarius[99] rather than Scotus.[100]

It is well known that our dogmas have not always been properly explained, nor universally received in our Church. As Jesus Christ did not inform us in what manner the Holy Ghost operated, for a long time the Latin Church believed, along with the Greek, that it operated only through God the Father; later, they added that it could also work through God the Son. Let me ask this: if the day after this decision was taken a citizen continued to recite the Creed of the day before, would he merit the death penalty? Are cruelty and injustice less heinous when they inflict punishment today upon a man who thinks as we all used to think yesterday? At the time of Honorius I,[101] was a man sunk in guilt because he did not believe that Jesus was two wills in one?

It is not so long ago that the dogma of the Immaculate Conception was established; the Dominicans still refuse to believe it. At what point exactly will the Dominicans start deserving death in this world and damnation in the next?

If there is anyone to whom we should turn for guidance in our interminable disputes, it is certainly to the apostles and the evangelists. There was difference enough between St Peter and St Paul to provoke a violent schism. In his Epistle to the Galatians[102] Paul expressly states that he resisted Peter to his face, because he thought him deserving of reproach. Peter had been guilty with Barnabas of deceit; they had both dined with the Gentiles before the arrival of James, then

---

[97] Ratramnus was a Benedictine monk at Corbie, near Amiens, who died about 868. His fame rests upon a treatise on the Eucharist (*De corpore et sanguine Domini liber*) in which he argued against the doctrine of transubstantiation as promulgated by his contemporary Radbertus. This book remained on the Catholic index of prohibited works from 1559 to 1900.

[98] Radbertus Paschasius was born near Soissons and died about 860. He became a monk at Corbie, near Amiens, and taught a number of distinguished ecclesiastics.

[99] Berengarius was an eleventh-century French theologian, who repudiated the doctrine put forward by Radbertus because it was contrary to reason and therefore irreconcilable with the truthfulness of God – in other words it invited the faithful to believe something manifestly silly; it was also in opposition to the teachings of Augustine, Ambrose and Jerome; and it was unwarranted by Scripture.

[100] This is a misleading reference. The person intended is not Duns Scotus, who argued with Thomas Aquinas two centuries later, but John the Scot, otherwise known as Johannes Scotus Erigena. Erigena was a scholar and theologian, but even his dates, *c.* 800–77, make him unlikely to be in dispute with Berengarius, and in any case he advanced views very similar to those later voiced by Berengarius (i.e. that bread and wine are not *literally* body and blood).

[101] The son of a Roman consul, Honorius I was Pope from 625 to 638, and allied himself with the Monothelites in their view that Christ was 'one will', for which he was condemned forty years after his death.

[102] 2:11–14.

51

slunk away furtively, deserting the Gentiles for fear of offending the circumcised. 'When I found', said Paul, 'that they were not following the true path of the Gospel, I said to Cephas [Peter][103] in front of them all: Since thou, who art born a Jew, dost follow the Gentile, not the Jewish way of life, by what right dost thou bind the Gentiles to live like Jews?'

There was matter here for an acrimonious quarrel. The question was: should the new Christians observe Jewish ceremonies, or should they not? At this very time, St Paul was wont to go and sacrifice in the temple of Jerusalem. We know that the first fifteen Bishops of Jerusalem were circumcised Jews, who observed the sabbath and abstained from forbidden meat. Now, if a Spanish or Portuguese bishop were to have himself circumcised and to observe the Jewish sabbath he would be burnt at the stake in an *auto-da-fé*. And yet this fundamental point failed to cause the slightest dissension among either the apostles or the first Christians.

Had the evangelists been anything like modern writers, they would have had masses of opportunity to squabble amongst themselves. St Matthew counts twenty-eight generations from David to Jesus. St Luke counts forty-one. Moreover, Luke's generations are absolutely different from Matthew's. But no argument erupted between the disciples over these apparent contradictions, which were subsequently reconciled by several fathers of the Church. Feelings were not hurt; peace was preserved. There exists no greater example than this, to teach that we should be tolerant with one another in our disagreements and humble when faced with something we do not understand.

In his Epistle to some Jews of Rome who converted to Christianity, St Paul devotes the whole latter part of the third chapter to the proposition that one may attain Glory only through Faith, and that Works count for nothing. St James, on the other hand, in his Epistle to the twelve tribes scattered throughout the world, chapter 2, repeatedly states that one cannot find salvation without good works. And there we have the basis of one of the most severe divisions in our modern Church, over an issue which did not divide the apostles in any way.

If to persecute those with whom we disagree were a pious thing to do, it would follow that the man who managed to kill the greatest number of heretics would be the most holy saint in Paradise. What kind of impression would he make up there, who was merely content to ruin his brother men and throw them into dungeons, next to the fanatic who despatched hundreds to their deaths on the day of St Bartholomew? The answer is apparently as follows.

---

[103] Peter's original name was probably Simon. Jesus gave him his new name, derived from the Aramaic word *kepa* (for 'rock'). 'Cephas' is the Greek phonetic transliteration of this word, and was used more commonly than 'Peter' in the primitive Church. 'Peter' ultimately prevailed, as it is the Greek translation of the meaning of the word (and not just the sound) which would have told early Christians far more about the man than 'Cephas'.

The successors of St Peter and his consistory cannot make mistakes. They approved, celebrated, even consecrated the massacre of St Bartholomew. Therefore this was a very sacred act. Therefore also, of two murderers equal in piety, the one who disembowelled twenty-four pregnant Huguenot women must be promoted to double the amount of beatitude over the one who ripped open only twelve. By the same reckoning, the fanatics of the Cévennes must have calculated that they would be elevated in glory in exact proportion to the number of priests, monks and Catholic women they were able to slaughter. These are strange claims indeed to eternal glory.

12

Whether religious persecution was part of the divine law in Judaism, and whether it was always practised

By *divine law* we mean, I believe, those precepts handed down by God himself. He commanded that Jews should eat a lamb cooked with lettuce, and that guests should eat it standing up, rod in hand, in memory of the Passover; He ordered that the High Priest should be consecrated by putting blood on his right ear, his right hand, and his right foot; both seem extraordinary customs to us, but they caused not a stir of surprise in Antiquity. God further required that the goat *Hazazel* should bear all the sins of the Jewish people, and He forbade the consumption of scale-less fish, pig, hare, hedgehog, owls, eagles, and so on.

He instituted festivals and ceremonies which,when viewed according to logic and custom, appeared totally arbitrary to other nations, yet because they were commanded by God Himself, they became Divine Law for the Jews, just as everything that Jesus Christ, the son of Mary and the son of God, has commanded us to do is now Divine Law for us.

We shall not examine here exactly why God should have substituted new laws to replace those he gave to Moses, nor why He should have given more commandments to Moses than to the patriarch Abraham, and more to Abraham than to Noah. It looks as if He adapts Himself to the times and to particular groups within the human race, according to a kind of paternal scale, but these profound mysteries are too obscure for our feeble intelligence to comprehend. Let us keep within the limits of our subject, and first take a look at the level of intolerance amongst the ancient Jews.

It is true that in Exodus, Numbers, Leviticus and Deuteronomy there is mention of very severe religious laws and even severer penalties. Many commentators have had difficulty reconciling the account of Moses with certain

54

passages in Jeremiah and Amos, and especially with the famous discourse of St Stephen as related in the Acts of the Apostles. Amos says that in the wilderness the Jews continued to worship Moloch, Remphan and Chiun.[104] Jeremiah categorically states that God required no sacrifices from their forefathers when they were led out of Egypt.[105] St Stephen, in his speech to the Jews, expresses himself thus: 'They worshipped the host of Heaven, neither they offered sacrifices nor oblations in the wilderness for forty years, but carried the tabernacle of the god Moloch and the star of the god Remphan.'[106]

Other critics have inferred from this cult of so many strange gods that they were sanctioned by Moses, and they cite in support of their thesis these words from Deuteronomy, addressed to the Israelites: 'It will not be for every man, there as here, to worship when and where he pleases.'[107]

They rest this opinion upon the absence of any mention of religious acts by the Israelites when in the wilderness – no observation of the Passover, no Pentecost, no reference to the feast of the tabernacles, no established public worship; moreover, circumcision, that seal of the pact between God and Abraham, was not practised at all.

They find additional evidence in the story of Joshua, who told the Israelites: 'If it seem evil unto you to serve the Lord, choose you this day whom you will serve; whether the gods which your fathers served in Mesopotamia or the gods of the Amorites, in whose land ye dwell.' The people replied, 'Nay, but we will serve the Lord our God [Adonai]', to which Joshua said, 'Ye have chosen, now therefore put away the strange gods which are among you.' Scholars claim that this passage proves the Israelites, in the time of Moses, had other gods apart from Adonai.[108]

It would serve no purpose to refute here those critics who argue that the Pentateuch was not written by Moses. Everything that needed to be said on the subject was said long ago. And even if some tiny portion of the Book of Moses had been written at the time of the Judges, or the Kings, or the Prophets, that would not render it any less divinely inspired.[109]

---

[104] Amos, 5:26: 'But now you shall take up the shrine of your idol king, and the pedestals of your images, which you have made for yourselves, and I will drive you into exile beyond Damascus' (New English Bible). Remphan and Chiun are interchangeable readings for the same word. The meaning of the passage has been much disputed, and some scholars do not see it as Amos chiding the Israelites for worshipping false gods, but rather for the manner of their worship.

[105] Jeremiah, 7:22: 'But when I brought your forefathers out of Egypt, I gave them no commands about whole-offering and sacrifice; I said not a word about them.'

[106] Acts, 7:42–3.   [107] Deuteronomy, 12:8 (Vulgate).

[108] Joshua, 24:15–25. Adonai comes from the Canaanite and Hebrew word *adon*, which means 'lord'. Hence 'adonai', meaning 'my lord', is a substitute for 'Yahweh'.

[109] The first five books of the Old Testament were orally transmitted stories and legends which were not written down by dedicated scribes until post-exile, some thousand years after their supposed occurrence.

It is written in Holy Scripture, which seems to me proof enough, that despite the singular punishment visited upon the Jews for their worship of the Golden Calf, they preserved complete liberty of conscience for a very long period. It might even be that the massacre Moses inflicted upon twenty-three thousand men as punishment for the exaltation of this idol by his brother Aaron, made him finally realise that, in matters of religion, nothing was achieved by harshness, and he was thereafter obliged to turn a blind eye to people's enthusiasm for peculiar gods.

He himself seems to have transgressed his own laws at a very early stage. He forbids false images, yet erects a bronze statue of the serpent.[110] There is later evidence of the same exception to Mosaic law in the temple of Solomon, who had a dozen oxen sculpted to support the great font of the temple; two-headed cherubim (one an eagle and the other a calf) were placed in the ark; and it was apparently this poorly executed head of a calf which for a long time convinced the Roman soldiers who came upon it that the Jews were worshippers of an ass.[111]

In vain was the cult of false images prohibited; Solomon pursued his idolatry in peace. Jeroboam, to whom God gave ten parts of the kingdom, erected two golden calves[112] and reigned for twenty-two years, uniting in his person the twin dignities of monarch and high priest. The diminutive Kingdom of Judah, under Rehoboam, built altars and carved statues to strange gods; the good King Asa made no attempt to destroy any of the holy sites. The high priest Uriah replaced the temple's altar for burnt offerings with another given to him by the King of Assyria. In a word, there is no sign of any constraint whatever being placed upon religious worship. I am aware that most of the kings of Israel exterminated and assassinated each other, but in every case it was for political motives and not for reasons of religious belief.

It is true that there were some among the prophets who called upon Heaven to avenge them. Elijah brought down heavenly fire to consume the priests of Baal. Elisha summoned bears to devour forty-two little children who had drawn impudent attention to his bald pate. But these are somewhat uncommon miracles, and the events themselves might prove hard to reproduce.

Another objection often heard is that the Jewish people were very ignorant and barbarous. It is said that in the war against the Madianites Moses ordered every male child and every mother to be murdered, and their spoils to be divided.[113] In the field the conquerors found six hundred and seventy-five

---

[110] Numbers, 21:9: 'So Moses made a bronze serpent and erected it as a standard, so that when a snake had bitten a man, he could look at the bronze serpent and recover.'

[111] 2 Chronicles, 4.   [112] 1 Kings, 12:28.

[113] Madian was not included in the Promised Land: it is a small canton of Idumea in Arabia Petrea, extending from the torrent of Arnon in the north to that of Zared in the midst of rocks on the eastern side of Lake Asphaltis. This country is at present inhabitated by a small Arabian

thousand lambs, seventy-two thousand oxen, sixty-one thousand asses, and thirty-two thousand young virgins; they shared out what they wanted and slew the rest. Several commentators go so far as to claim that thirty-two of the maidens were burnt in sacrifice to God: *Cesserunt in partem Domini triginta duae animae.*[114]

Yes indeed, the Israelites did sacrifice human beings to the Deity, as witness the daughter of Jephthah, and King Agag, cut to pieces by the prophet Samuel. To encourage them, Ezekiel himself promises that they will eat human flesh. 'You will eat the horse and the horseman', he says, 'you will drink the blood of princes.' Some commentators have applied two couplets of this prophecy to the Israelites themselves, and the remainder to carnivorous animals.[115] Throughout the history of the Jews you will find not one instance of generosity, magnanimity or charity; and yet, in the fog of this long and frightful barbarism, one may always discern rays of universal tolerance.

Jephthah, who sacrificed his daughter under the influence of divine inspiration, said to the Amorites: 'Wilt thou not possess that which Kemosh thy god giveth thee to possess? So whomsoever the Lord our God shall drive from before us, them will we possess.'[116] This statement is precise; it could lead to much; but at the very least it offers evident proof that God tolerated Kemosh. For the Holy Scripture does not say, 'You think you have the right to lands which you claim were given to you by the god Kemosh'; it says very clearly, 'You have the right', *tibi jure debentur*, which is the real meaning of the original Hebrew words, *Otho thirasch*.

The story of Micah and the Levite, in the seventeenth and eighteenth chapters of the Book of Judges, provides yet another irrefutable proof of the unlimited tolerance and widest possible liberty then obtaining among the Jews. Micah's mother, a very rich woman from Mount Ephraim, had lost eleven hundred pieces of silver, and her son, who had taken them, gave them all back to her; she then dedicated this money to the Lord God and made idols of it and built a little chapel to house it. A Levite looked after the chapel in return for ten pieces of silver a year, a tunic, an overcoat and his food. And Micah said, 'Now God will look with favour upon me, for I have in my house a Levite priest.'[117]

In the meantime, six hundred men of the tribe of Dan were looking for a village in the area to take over, so they could establish themselves there. Having no Levite priest at hand, and needing the blessing of God for their enterprise, they went to Micah's house and made off with his ephod, his silver idols and his

tribe, and may be about eight leagues or so in length and somewhat less in breadth. [Voltaire's note]
[114] Numbers, 31:3–48. 'The Lord's tribute was thirty-and-two persons' (verse 40).
[115] Ezekiel, 39:18–20.   [116] Judges, 11:24.   [117] Judges, 17.

57

Levite, despite the latter's remonstrances and the protestations of Micah and his mother. They then went forth boldly to attack the city of Laish, which they put to fire and the sword according to their custom. They renamed the city *Dan* to commemorate their victory, and placed Micah's idol on an altar. What is even more remarkable, Jonathan, the grandson of Moses, was the high priest of this temple, wherein thenceforth the God of Israel and the idol of Micah were both worshipped.[118]

After the death of Gideon the Hebrews renounced God and worshipped Baal-Berith for nigh on twenty years, without any chief, judge or priest crying out for vengeance against them. Their crime was great, I admit, but if even this idolatry was tolerated, how many deviations within the true faith must there have been?

Some have cited the incident when the Lord God himself allowed the Ark[119] to be taken in battle by the Philistines, and inflicted only slight punishment upon them, namely to strike them with a mysterious malady resembling piles, to topple the statue of Dagon, and to send a plague of rats into their lands. But when, to appease his wrath, the Philistines returned the Ark harnessed to two cows feeding their calves, and made him an offering of five golden rats and five golden haemorrhoids, the Lord God put to death seventy of the ancients of Israel and fifty thousand of the people, for the mere act of having looked upon the Ark. This is given as proof of intolerance. The reply to which is that the Lord's anger was not occasioned by a belief, by a difference of fashion within a belief, nor by any idolatry.

Had he intended to punish idolatry, the Lord God would have put to death all the Philistines who had stolen his Ark and who worshipped Dagon; instead, he killed fifty thousand and seventy men of his own people, for the sole reason that they had looked upon the Ark which they should not have seen at all; so much do ancient Jewish laws, customs and economy differ from anything we know today, and so much also are the inscrutable ways of God above any of our own! Says the judicious Dr Calmet,[120] 'The severity used against this great number will appear excessive only to those who fail to understand how far God wished to be feared and respected among his people, or who judge the intentions and opinions of God according to the feeble light of their human reason.'[121]

God did not, therefore, punish the worship of false gods, but rather a profanation of his own worship, an unwise display of curiosity, an act of disobedience, perhaps even a spirit of revolt. We must recognise that punish-

[118] Judges, 18.
[119] The Ark of the Covenant, the sacred chest of acacia wood overlaid with gold which the Israelites took with them on their journey into Palestine.
[120] Antoine Augustin Calmet (1672–1757), Benedictine scholar, chiefly known for his *Histoire ecclésiastique et civile de la Lorraine* (1728).
[121] From Calmet's *Commentaire de la Bible* (1707–16, in 23 volumes).

ments such as these belong to God only in Jewish theocracy. We cannot state too often that customs which occur in the Old Testament bear little resemblance to those of our own day.

When, in later times, the idolater Naaman asked Elisha whether he could follow his king into the temple of Rimmon and worship there with him, did not this Elisha, the same who had fed little children to the bears for having mocked him, reply, 'Go in peace'?[122]

There is much more: the Lord commands Jeremiah to place ropes on his neck, to make bonds and yokes, and to send them to the princes of Moab, Ammon, Edom, Tyre and Sidon, and has Jeremiah say to them, 'I have delivered all your lands into the hands of Nebuchadnezzar, King of Babylon, my servant.' Here we have an idolatrous king declared to be the servant and favourite of God.

The same Jeremiah whom the Jewish princeling Zedekiah had thrown into a dungeon, having obtained Zedekiah's pardon, then advises him on behalf of God to submit himself to the King of Babylon. 'If you surrender to his officers', he says, 'your soul will be saved.' So God takes sides with an idolatrous king.[123] Furthermore, he gives him the Ark, the mere sight of which had cost the lives of fifty thousand and seventy Israelites. He delivers up to him the holy of holies and the rest of the temple to build which had cost a hundred and eight thousand gold talents, one million and seventeen thousand silver talents, and six thousand gold drachmas, all left by David and his representatives for the construction of the house of God; the which, not counting the monies spent by Solomon, amounts to nineteen thousand and seventy millions, or thereabouts, in today's currency. Never did idolatry receive greater reward. I realise that this calculation is probably exaggerated, that there are errors in transcription, but even if you reduce it to half its size, or a quarter, or an eighth, it is still an astonishing figure. One is hardly less impressed by the riches which Herodotus says he saw in the temple at Ephesus. Of course, treasures are as nothing to God, and the only real treasure in this story, an inestimable one, was the title of servant which he gave to Nebuchadnezzar.

God showed no less partiality to the Kir, or Koresh, whom we call Cyrus. He calls him his *Christ*, his *Anointed*, although he was not anointed according to the usual meaning of the word but followed the religion of Zoroaster; and he calls him his *shepherd*, although he was an usurper in the eyes of the world; there is no greater mark of favour in the whole of Holy Scripture.[124]

You will find, in Malachi, that 'from the rising to the setting of the sun the

---

[122] 2 Kings, 5:17–19. The two books of Samuel are sometimes referred to as 1 and 2 Kings, so that the two books of Kings become 3 and 4 Kings. Such is the numbering followed by the Pléiade edition of Voltaire, but here we follow the New English Bible.

[123] Jeremiah, 27:6, 17.   [124] Isaiah, 24 and 25.

name of God is great throughout the world and that everywhere he is given the purest offerings'.[125] God takes care of the idolatrous Ninevites just as he takes care of the Jews; he threatens them, and he forgives them. Melchizedek, who was not Jewish, was nonetheless a priest of God. Balaam the idolator was a prophet. Scripture therefore teaches us that not only did God tolerate other religions, but that he bestowed his paternal benevolence upon them all. And still we dare to be intolerant!

[125] Malachi, 1:11.

13
The extraordinary tolerance of the Jews

And so under Moses, under the Judges, under the Kings, one continually finds examples of tolerance. There is yet more: several times Moses says that 'God will visit the sins of the fathers upon the children, even unto the fourth generation.' The threat was necessary for a people to whom God had revealed neither the immortality of the soul nor the rewards and trials of the afterlife. These truths are absent from the Decalogue and are not referred to in any law of Leviticus or Deuteronomy. They constituted dogma for the Persians, the Babylonians, the Egyptians, the Greeks, the Cretans, but they played no part in the religion of the Jews. Moses does not say, 'Honour thy father and thy mother, if thou wilt go to Heaven', but 'Honour thy father and thy mother, that thy days may be long in the land which the Lord thy God giveth thee', i.e. in *this* life. His threats are all to do with corporeal ailments or material loss – scurvy, abscesses, malignant ulcers on the knee or the calf, a wife's infidelity, borrowing from usurers and being unable to lend with interest, starving to death or being obliged to eat one's own children. But at no point does he tell them that their immortal souls will suffer torments after death, or will enjoy eternal happiness. God led his people himself, and issued punishment for bad acts and reward for good acts with immediate effect. Everything was temporal; and this the learned Bishop Warburton[126] advances as proof positive that Jewish laws were of divine origin, because God himself being their King and dispensing justice on the spot, he had no need to devise and reveal a doctrine which would be brought into play when he no longer governed his

---

[126] William Warburton, Bishop of Gloucester (1698–1779). Voltaire here refers to Warburton's book *The Divine Legation of Moses demonstrated on the Principles of a Religious Deist* (1737–41), which caused fierce controversy. Warburton answers the Deists' charge that Mosaic law was not divinely inspired because it made no mention of an afterlife, with the bold paradox that only God would have dared omit such an important consideration.

people. Those who ignorantly claim that Moses taught the immortality of the soul remove from the New Testament one of its greatest advantages over the Old. It is an established fact that the Law of Moses gave notice only of temporal punishments unto the fourth generation. However, despite the precise wording of this law, despite the express declaration of God that He would inflict punishment unto the fourth generation, we find Ezekiel telling the Jews exactly the opposite – that the son will not inherit the sins of the father;[127] he goes so far as to have God say that he had given them statutes that were not good.[128]

The Book of Ezekiel was nonetheless admitted into the canon of writers inspired by God. True, boys under thirteen were not allowed to read it in the synagogue, as St Jerome tells us; but that was for fear they might be corrupted by the excessively vivid account of the licentious behaviour of the sisters Aholah and Aholibah. In short, Ezekiel's book was always accepted as canonical, notwithstanding its clear refutation of Moses.

Finally, when the immortality of the soul became received dogma, which was probably around the time of the Babylonish captivity, the Sadducees continued to believe that there were no punishments or rewards after death, and that our sentient and sapient faculties died with us in much the same way as our mobile faculty – the ability to walk and propel oneself. They denied the existence of angels. They were much more different from other Jews than Protestants are from Catholics. But that did not exclude them from communion with their brothers; there were even some high priests from among their sect.

The Pharisees believed in predestination[129] and the transmigration of

[127] Ezekiel, 18:20.

[128] Ezekiel, 20:25. This opinion of Ezekiel was at length the prevailing one in the synagogue; but there were always some Jews who, while they believed in eternal punishment, also believed that God punished the sins of the fathers upon their children. At present they are punished even beyond the fiftieth generation, and are still in danger of eternal punishment. It may be asked how the offspring of those Jews who were not involved in putting Christ to death, such as those in Jerusalem who had no hand in the affair, as well as others scattered all over the earth, can be temporally punished in the persons of their children who were as innocent as their fathers. This temporal punishment, or rather this manner of being so different from other peoples and of carrying on trade without having a country of their own, this cannot be considered as a punishment when it is compared to what they are to expect on account of their unbelief, which they may avoid by a sincere repentance. [Voltaire's note]

[129] The doctrine of predestination is both ancient and universal: we find it constantly in Homer. Jupiter wanted to save the life of his son Sarpedon: but Destiny had sentenced him to die, and Jupiter was obliged to submit. For the philosophers, destiny was that chain of causes and effects necessarily produced by nature, or that same necessary chain ordained by Providence – which is much more reasonable. The whole system of fatality is contained in the following line of Seneca: 'Ducant volentem fata, nolentem trahunt.' It has always been acknowledged that God governs the universe by eternal, universal and immutable laws: this truth gave rise to the many unintelligible disputes concerning free will, because nobody had defined the term liberty before the great philosopher Locke. He proved that liberty was no more than the power to act. God has given man this power, and man, acting freely in accordance with the eternal decrees of Providence, is one of the wheels of the great machine of the universe. Free will has been a matter

souls.[130] The Essenes thought that the souls of the good went to the Happy Isles[131] and those of the bad to a kind of Tartarus. They offered no sacrifices, and met in a special synagogue apart from the others. In a word, if one is prepared to examine Judaism closely, one will be surprised to find, in the midst of barbaric horrors, the most extraordinary spirit of tolerance. Yes, it is a paradox, but then nearly all people have been governed by some measure of contradiction; happy are those whose society is gentle though their laws be bloody.

for dispute since Antiquity, but no one has been persecuted on account of it until recently. How horrible, how absurd it is to have imprisoned on this account an Arnauld, a Sacy, a Nicole and so many other luminaries in France! [Voltaire's note]

[130] The theological romance of the transmigration of souls came from India, a part of the world from which we have received many more fables than is commonly supposed. This doctrine is admirably explained in the fifteenth book of Ovid's *Metamorphoses*. It has been received in almost every part of the world, and has everywhere met with opposition: but we have never heard of any priest among the ancients causing a disciple of Pythagoras to be sent to prison. [Voltaire's note]

[131] Neither the ancient Jews, nor the Egyptians, nor the Greeks, their contemporaries, believed that the soul of man went to heaven after death. The Jews thought that the sun and the moon moved in the same orbit a few leagues above our heads, and that the firmament was a thick and solid vault, which supported the weight of the waters that sometimes escaped through little cracks. The ancient Greeks placed the palace of their Gods on Mount Olympus. And, in Homer's time, the abode of heroes after death was thought to be on an island beyond the ocean. This was also the opinion of the Essenes. Since the time of Homer the planets have been assigned to the Gods, but there was no more reason for men to place a god on the moon than for the inhabitants of the moon to place a god on our planet. Juno and Iris had no other palace but the clouds, where they had no place to rest their feet. Among the Sabeans every deity had its star. But as the stars are little suns, it would be impossible to live there unless you were made of fire itself. It is therefore quite pointless to enquire what the ancients thought of heaven: the best answer that can be given is that they had no idea at all. [Voltaire's note]

14
Whether Jesus Christ preached tolerance

Let us now see if Jesus Christ established any bloodthirsty laws, or commanded his followers to be intolerant, or built torture-chambers, or instituted the butchery of the *auto-da-fé*.

Unless I am mistaken, there are very few passages in the gospels which a prejudiced mind might interpret as legitimising intolerance and constraint. One of them is the parable in which the Kingdom of Heaven is compared to a king who invites guests to the wedding-feast of his son and has his servants deliver this message: 'I have prepared my feast, the oxen have been killed, and the fatlings, all is ready now; come to the wedding.'[132] Some ignore the invitation and depart for their houses in the country, others are unimpressed and go about their business, yet others insult the king by killing his servants. The king sends his armies against these murderers and destroys their city, then invites to his feast every single person his servants can find on the open road. One of these, having neglected to wear an appropriate nuptial garment at table, was bound hand and foot and cast into outer darkness.

It is obvious that, since this allegory only applies to the Kingdom of Heaven, no man should consider it gives him licence to throttle or imprison any guest who has the mischance to turn up for dinner in the wrong clothes; and I know of no case in history of a prince hanging a courtier over such a trifle; nor is it to be feared that when an emperor, having already killed his chickens, sends pages to far-flung princes of the empire to invite them to dinner, the said princes will murder the said pages. The meaning of the allegory is allusive: the invitation to the feast stands for the preaching of the

---

[132] Matthew, 22:4.

gospel; the killing of the messengers signifies persecution against those who preach wisdom and virtue.

The other parable concerns the man who invites his friends to a grand dinner, and as soon as he is ready to sit down and eat, sends his servant to advise them. One friend excuses himself on the grounds that he has bought some land and must go and visit it; this does not appear to be a valid excuse, for one does not generally visit one's land in the dark. Another says he has bought five yoke of oxen and he has got to try them out; he is as reprehensible as the first, as it is unusual to exercise oxen when it is time for dinner. A third replies that he has just been married, which is a perfectly good excuse. The host, hopping mad, summons blind people and cripples to his banquet; then, seeing that there are still some empty places, he says to his manservant, 'Go out on to the highways and along the hedgerows and make them come in.'[133]

It is, in truth, not expressly stated that this parable refers to the Kingdom of Heaven. Too much has been made of the words 'make them come in'. But it stands to reason that a single manservant cannot prevail by force upon everyone he comes across to compel them to dine with his master; besides which, guests invited on such terms are unlikely to improve the geniality of the occasion. According to the most reliable commentators, '*make* them come in' means no more than 'ask, implore, entreat, desire' them to come in. What on earth, I ask you, has this request and this dinner to do with the subject of persecution?

If we construe this story literally, does it mean that we have to be blind, lame, and dragged by the nose in order to enter the bosom of the Church? Jesus says in the same parable, 'When thou makest a dinner or a supper, call not thy friends, nor thy brethren, nor thy rich kinsmen.'[134] Has anyone ever inferred from this that it is quite wrong to dine with one's family or friends as soon as they come into a little money?

After the parable of the feast, Christ says, 'If any man come to me, and hate not his father and mother, his wife and children, his brethren and sisters, yea, and his own life also, he cannot be my disciple' etc. 'For who is there among you who, wishing to build a tower, does not first compute the cost?'[135] Is there anyone in the world so perverse as to conclude from this that one should hate one's father and mother? Is it not easy enough to see that these words mean 'Do not weigh your love for me against the love you bear those dearest to you'?

There is a passage from St Matthew which is often quoted: 'Whosoever heareth not the word of God shall be like to an heathen, and like one who sitteth at the seat of custom.'[136] Now this does not mean that we should go about persecuting nonbelievers and tax-gatherers; they may be damned, yes, but they

---

[133] Luke, 14:23.   [134] Luke, 14:12.   [135] Luke, 14:25–9.   [136] Matthew, 18:17.

are not to be handed over to the secular power. Far from depriving the tax-gatherers of any of their rights as citizens, they have been accorded the highest privileges; theirs is the only profession to receive blanket damnation in Holy Scripture, and it is also the one most favoured by governments. Why then cannot we lavish as much forgiveness upon our brother who strays from the path as we do upon our brother who collects the taxes?

Another passage which has been grossly misinterpreted is that from St Matthew[137] and St Mark,[138] wherein it is said that Christ, being hungry one morning, approached a fig-tree and found it full of leaves only, as the season for figs had not yet arrived. He thereupon cursed the fig-tree, which immediately dried up.

Several different explanations for this miracle have been given; but could any one of them be used to justify persecution? A fig-tree has proved unable to yield fruit at the beginning of March, and it has been blasted. Is that good reason to blast our fellow men with pain and torment all year round? Let us treat with due reverence those parts of the Scriptures with which our vain, inquisitive minds have difficulty, and not use them as an excuse for implacable hatreds.

The spirit of intolerance, which distorts everything, has also contrived to find its justification in both the story of the tradesmen thrown out of the temple, and in that of the demons which Jesus expelled from the body of a man possessed and sent to inhabit instead the bodies of two thousand unclean animals. But is there anyone who cannot see that these two examples merely show God directly meting justice in response to a contravention of His law? It showed lack of respect for the house of the Lord to turn it into a street market. The Sanhedrin and priests might allow buying and selling to take place in order to facilitate the purchase of sacrifices to God; but the God to whom these sacrifices were offered might equally well decide, albeit in human guise, to demolish this profanity. By the same token, He was quite able to punish the farmers who introduced entire herds into the country, in violation of a law which He Himself observed. Examples such as these have nothing whatever to do with religious persecution. The spirit of intolerance must depend upon very poor evidence indeed, because it is always on the look-out for the most trivial pretexts, and because every other word and act of Christ exhorts patience, gentleness and forgiveness. Witness the father who welcomes back the prodigal son;[139] the labourer who arrives at the last moment but is paid the same as the others;[140] the good Samaritan;[141] Christ himself telling the disciples they need not fast;[142] he forgives the sinners;[143] to the woman taken in adultery he simply recommends she be faithful in future;[144] he even indulges the harmless enjoyment of the guests at Cana, who being already well warmed with wine ask for

[137] Matthew, 21:19–21. [138] Mark, 11:13–14. [139] Luke, 15. [140] Matthew, 20.
[141] Luke, 10. [142] Matthew, 9. [143] Luke, 7. [144] John, 8.

more; he is quite willing to perform a miracle for them, and turn their water into wine.[145]

He does not turn against Judas, who (he already knows) will betray him; he tells Peter to put away his sword;[146] he reprimands the children of Zebedee who, in imitation of Elias, tried to call upon heavenly fire to destroy a city which would not offer them lodging.[147]

In a word, Christ died a victim of malice. Should we venture to compare the sacred with the profane, and God with a mere mortal, his death from a human point of view is not unlike the death of Socrates. The Greek philosopher was sacrificed to the hatred of the sophists, the priests, and the leaders of the people; the Christian law-giver succumbed beneath the hatred of the scribes, the Pharisees, and the priests. Socrates could have avoided death, but chose not to; Jesus offered himself voluntarily. The Greek philosopher not only forgave his accusers and those iniquitous men who sat in judgement upon him, but even invited them to treat his children as they had treated himself, in the event his children might be fortunate enough to deserve their hatred; Jesus Christ, infinitely greater, asked his Father to forgive his enemies.[148]

If Jesus Christ seemed to fear death, if his agony was so extreme as to draw from him sweat mixed with blood[149] – a very rare and violent symptom – it is because he wished to humble himself so far as to experience all the weakness of the human form he had assumed. His body shook, and his soul did not flinch. He was teaching us that true strength, true greatness consisted in enduring all the miseries which afflict the human condition. There is extreme courage in embracing death even as one is terrified of it.

Socrates had chided the sophists with their ignorance and had convicted them of falsehood. Christ, with divine right, treated the scribes and Pharisees as hypocrites, blinkered fools, vicious sinners, a race of vipers.[150]

Socrates was never accused of wanting to establish a new religion. Neither was Christ; we are told that the high priests and the entire council had to seek false witness against him in order to ensure his death.[151]

So, if they had to seek false witnesses, they did not reproach him with having publicly preached against legal authority. In fact, he was subject to the laws of Moses from his infancy until the day he died; he had been circumcised on the eighth day like every other Jewish child. He was subsequently baptised in the River Jordan, but that was according to a ceremony sacred to Jews and to all the peoples of the east; all recognised impurities were cleansed by baptism; priests

---

[145] John, 2:9. [146] Matthew, 26:52. [147] Luke, 9:55.

[148] Luke, 23:34: 'Father, forgive them, for they know not what they do.' [149] Luke, 22:44.

[150] Matthew, 23.

[151] Matthew, 26:59: 'The chief priests and the whole Council tried to find some allegation against Jesus on which a death-sentence could be based; but they failed to find one, though many came forward with false evidence' (New English Bible).

were consecrated in the same way, being plunged into water at the feast of solemn expiation, and proselytes were similarly baptised.

Jesus observed all points of the law. He regularly kept the Sabbath. He abstained from forbidden meats. He celebrated all the festivals; just before his death he had celebrated Passover. He was not accused of having advanced any new opinion, nor of having observed any strange rite. Born a Jew, it was as a Jew that he led his entire life.

Two witnesses came forward to accuse him of having said that he could destroy the temple and rebuild it in three days.[152] Such a claim was totally incomprehensible to ordinary Jews, so it did not amount to an accusation of having wanted to establish a new sect.

The high priest questioned him. 'I command you', he said, 'in the name of the living God, to tell us if you are Christ the Son of God.'[153] We are not told what the high priest meant by the words 'Son of God'. The expression was sometimes used to indicate a good person,[154] just as 'son of Belial' indicated a bad person. At any rate, the coarse Jews had not the smallest conception of the sacred mystery of a Son of God, being God Himself, coming upon earth.

Jesus answered, 'Thou hast said; nevertheless, I say unto you, hereafter shall ye see the Son of man sitting on the right hand of the power of God, and coming in the clouds of Heaven.'[155]

This reply was regarded by the Sanhedrin as blasphemous. As the Sanhedrin no longer had power to execute, they took Jesus before the Roman governor of the province and falsely accused him of having disturbed the peace by telling his people they did not need to pay taxes to Caesar and by claiming to be King of the Jews. There is, then, the best possible evidence that he was accused of offences against the State.

The governor Pilate, having learnt that he was from Galilee, initially sent him to appear before Herod, the tetrarch. Herod thought it impossible that Jesus could have really aspired to being a political leader or a royal claimant and treated him with ridicule. He sent him back to Pilate, who with contemptible cowardice sentenced him to death in order to appease the baying of the multitude. And this despite his having already once experienced a Jewish

---

[152] Matthew, 26:61.   [153] Matthew, 26:63.

[154] It was virtually impossible for the Jews to comprehend, without the intercession of specific revelation, the unfathomable mystery of the incarnation of the Son of God, God Himself. In Genesis, chapter 6, 'sons of God' refers to the sons of influential men; similarly, the cedars in the Psalms [79:11] are called 'cedars of God', and Saul's unhappiness is termed the 'melancholy of God'. It seems, however, that the Jews realised that Jesus called himself the Son of God in the proper sense; and if they considered these words to be blasphemous, that is perhaps yet another proof of the ignorance wherein they languished with regard to the mystery of the Incarnation, and to the coming of the Son of God, sent to earth for the salvation of mankind. [Voltaire's note]

[155] Matthew, 26:64.

rebellion, if we are to believe Josephus. Pilate did not show the same generosity as the governor Festus did at a later date.[156]

I will now enquire whether it is tolerance which is divinely ordained, or intolerance. If you want to be like Jesus Christ, better be a martyr than a hangman.

[156] Acts, 25:16.

15
Authorities against persecution

In matters of religion, it is impious to rob men of their liberty, to prevent them from choosing their deity. No man, and no god, would wish for an enforced adherence. (*Apologeticum*, Ch. 24)

If violence were employed to defend the faith, the bishops would oppose it. (St Hilarius, Bk I)

Enforced religion is no religion at all; the essence is to persuade, not compel. Religion cannot be adopted on command. (Lactantius, Bk III)

It is an abominable heresy to try to compel by force, by beatings, by imprisonment, those whom one has failed to convince by argument. (St Athanasius, Bk I)

Nothing is more contrary to the spirit of religion than coercion. (St Justin the Martyr, Bk v)

Is it for us to persecute those whom God tolerates? – so said St Augustine, before his quarrel with the Donatists made him too severe.

Let there be no violence done to the Jews! (4th Council of Toledo, 56th canon)

Advise but do not compel. (Letter of St Bernard)

We do not pretend to dispel error by violence. (Discourse of the Clergy of France to Louis XIII)

We have always disapproved of rigorous measures. (Assembly of the Clergy, 11 August 1560)

We know that faith comes through persuasion and not by order. (Fléchier, Bishop of Nîmes, Letter xix)

We should even guard against using language which might affront. (Bishop Du Bellay, in a pastoral letter)

Chapter 15

Remember that afflictions of the soul cannot be cured by constraint or violence. (Cardinal Le Camus, pastoral instruction of 1688)

Civil tolerance must be granted to all. (Fénelon, Archbishop of Cambrai, to the Duke of Burgundy)

The enforced adherence to a religion is clear proof that the spirit which moves it is inimical to the truth. (Dirois, a doctor of the Sorbonne, Bk vi, Ch. 4)

Violence creates hypocrites. You cannot hope to persuade when you hurl threats all over the place. (Tillemont, *Ecclesiastical History*, Vol. vi)

It seemed to us consistent with fairness and common sense to follow in the footsteps of the early Church, which never used force to establish and spread the faith. (Remonstrance of the Parliament of Paris to Henri II)

Experience teaches us that violence is more likely to exacerbate than to cure a sickness which has its root in the mind. (De Thou, *Epistle dedicated to Henri IV*)

Faith cannot be inspired at the point of a sword. (Cerisiers, *On the reigns of Henri IV and Louis XIII*)

It is a barbaric zeal which claims to implant religion in the hearts of men, as if conviction could result from enforcement. (Boulainvilliers, *The State of France*)

In religion as in love, a command is useless, and force even more so; there is nothing more independent of constraint than love and faith. (Amelot de la Houssaie, on the letters of Cardinal d'Ossat)

If Heaven has bestowed sufficient favour upon you to show you the truth, you are in a state of great grace; but must those who are heirs of their fathers hate those who are not? (Montesquieu, *On the Spirit of the Laws*, Bk xxv)

One could compile an enormous volume entirely filled with passages such as these. All our histories, speeches, sermons, moral tracts, catechisms, in our day breathe with the spirit of forbearance and teach it as a sacred duty. By what mischance or inconsistency should we belie in practice a sentiment which we proclaim every day? When our actions contradict our principles, it is because we think there is some advantage to us in doing the opposite of what we teach. But there is certainly no advantage in persecuting those who do not share our views and making ourselves hateful to them. Yet again, therefore, there is an inherent absurdity in intolerance. But, you will say, those whose business it is to restrain the consciences of others are by no means absurd. It is to them that the following little dialogue is addressed.

16
Conversation between a dying man and a man in good health

A man was on his deathbed in a provincial town; another man, hale and hearty, came to disturb his peace with these words:

Wretch! I want you now to think like me, sign this paper, and confess that there are five propositions in a book which neither of us have read; I want you to side with Lanfranc[157] against Bérenger,[158] and with St Thomas[159] against St Bonaventure;[160] I want you to embrace the second Council of Nicaea and reject the Council of Frankfurt; and I want you to explain to me how the words *My father is greater than myself*[161] come to mean *I am as great as he is.*

Tell me why the Father transmits every attribute to the Son, except paternity. If you don't, I shall have your body thrown on to the garbage-heap, your children will inherit nothing from you, your wife shall be deprived of her marriage portion, and your whole family will be driven to beg in the streets for bread, which I and those like me will refuse them.

The Dying Man: I barely understand what you are saying; the threats you make are all confused in my head; they trouble my soul and are turning my death into a nightmare. In the name of God, have pity!

The Wicked Man: Pity! I cannot have pity unless you agree with me in everything.

The Dying Man: Alas! You must know that all my senses are fading in these last moments of life, all the windows of my judgement are closing, my intel-

---

[157] Lanfranc (1005–89) was Archbishop of Canterbury at the time of William the Conqueror.
[158] See n. 99 above. [159] Thomas Aquinas (1225–74). [160] St Bonaventure (1221–74).
[161] John, 14:28.

lect is ebbing away, my mind grows dim. Am I in any state to argue with you?

The Wicked Man: All right! If you cannot believe what I want you to, say you believe it and that will suffice.

The Dying Man: How can I perjure myself just to please you? In a moment from now I shall appear before the God who punishes perjurers.

The Wicked Man: That doesn't matter; you will have the comfort of being buried in a cemetery, and your wife and children will have enough to live on. So die a hypocrite! Hypocrisy is a good thing; as someone said, it is the homage which vice pays to virtue.[162] My friend, a little hypocrisy costs you nothing.

The Dying Man: Alas! Either you scorn God, or you do not acknowledge Him, for you are asking me to tell a lie when I am at the point of death; you must soon receive your own judgement before Him, and you will have to answer for that lie.

The Wicked Man: What, you impudent wretch? I not acknowledge God?

The Dying Man: My brother, forgive me, but I fear you do not know Him. He whom I worship gives me renewed strength, at this very moment, to tell you with my dying breath that if you believe in God you must treat me with charity. He gave me my wife and children; do not make them die destitute. As for my body, do what you like with it, I surrender it to you. But believe in God, I implore you!

The Wicked Man: No more quibbling! Do as I say. I demand it, I order you.

The Dying Man: What good can it do you to torment me so?

The Wicked Man: What good, you ask? As soon as I have your signature, I shall be in line for a pretty good canonicate.

The Dying Man: Ah, dear brother! My last moment has come. I am dying. I shall pray God that He may touch your heart and convert you.

The Wicked Man: Damn the rogue, he didn't sign! I shall have to forge his signature and sign for him.

The following letter provides confirmation of the same moral values.

[162] Duc de la Rochefoucauld (1613–80), *Maximes*, 218.

17

Letter from a beneficed priest to the Jesuit, Father Le Tellier, on 6 May 1714

Reverend Father,[163]

In obedience to the orders received from Your Reverence, I have the honour to present before you the most sure methods of delivering Jesus and His society from their enemies. I estimate there are only about five hundred thousand Huguenots left in the kingdom, although some say a million and others fifteen hundred thousand; but however many there are, I humbly offer herewith my advice on what to do about them, which duty instructs me to submit to your superior judgement.

1. It would be a simple matter to round up all the preachers in one day and hang them together in the same place. Not only would this be good for the moral edification of the people, but it would make a fine spectacle.
2. I should have all heretical parents slaughtered in their beds, because to kill them in the streets might cause a riot; besides which, some of them might manage to escape, which must be avoided at all costs. These executions are a necessary corollary of our principles, for, as many great theologians have pointed out, if it is right and just to kill one heretic, it is obviously right and just to kill them all.
3. The following day I should have all the daughters of heretics married off to

[163] When this was written in 1762, the Jesuit order had not yet been abolished in France. Had they been victims of misfortune, I would certainly have given them my respect. But let no one ever forget that they were only persecuted because they had themselves been persecutors; and that the example they set may frighten even those who, being yet more intolerant than the Jesuits, hope one day to be able to oppress those of their fellow countrymen who do not share their harsh and ridiculous ideas. [Voltaire's note added in 1771]

74

good Catholics, it being understood that one must not depopulate the State too drastically after the last war; but with regard to boys of fourteen and fifteen, who are already polluted with dangerous ideas which we cannot hope to eradicate, my opinion is that they should all be castrated, in order that the breed should never reproduce. Younger boys will be educated in our colleges and flogged until they know the works of Sanchez[164] and Molina[165] by heart.

4. I also think, though I may be corrected, that we should apply the same measures to all the Lutherans in Alsace, in as much as I once saw two old Alsatian women in the year 1704 laughing on the day we were defeated at Hochstaedt.[166]

5. The question of the Jansenists might appear a little more awkward; I believe there must be at least six million of them; but a mind as noble as Your Reverence's will not be dismayed by this. I include amongst the Jansenists all those assemblies which so disgracefully uphold the freedom of the Gallican Church.[167] It is for Your Reverence, with customary wisdom, to weigh the various means of getting all these rebellious spirits to submit. The Gunpowder Plot was unsuccessful because one of the conspirators was so imprudent as to try to save the life of a friend; since you have no friend, we need not fear a like impediment; it would be a matter of the greatest ease for you to blow up all the parliaments in the realm with that invention of the monk Schwartz known as *pulvis pyrius*.[168] I have calculated that thirty-six barrels of gunpowder would be required for each parliament; so, if you multiply twelve parliaments by thirty-six barrels, you will see that we shall only need four hundred and thirty-two barrels, which, at one hundred écus each, adds up to one hundred and twenty-nine thousand six hundred pounds – a mere bagatelle for the Reverend Father-General. Once the parliaments have been blown up, you can pass their affairs over to your congregationists, who are perfectly well versed in the laws of the land.

6. It will be a simple matter to poison the Cardinal de Noailles, who is a guileless fellow with a trusting nature.

[164] Thomas Sanchez (1550–1610), Jesuit casuist from Cordova, author of *Disputationum de sancto matrimonii sacramento* (1592).

[165] Luis Molina (1535–1600), Spanish Jesuit whose philosophy is notable for its attempt to reconcile God's grace with predestination.

[166] Hochstaedt is the town in Bavaria where the Duke of Marlborough and Prince Eugene defeated the French in August 1704, in the Battle of Blenheim.

[167] The Gallican Church was stubbornly independent of the papacy. It upheld the right of French kings and clergy to act autonomously, without reference to the Pope, owing to their direct authority from God. They further claimed that the Pope's decisions were not valid until confirmed by his bishops.

[168] Berthold Schwartz (*c.* 1318–84), a Benedictine monk sometimes credited with the invention of gunpowder.

Your Reverence will have recourse to similar methods of conversion with regard to some refractory bishops, whose sees will be handed over to the Jesuits by means of a papal bull. As a result of which, all the bishops will be on the right side, and all the priests will have been cleverly chosen by the bishops. I should then proffer the following advice, pending Your Reverence's pleasure.

7. As the Jansenists are said at least to take Holy Communion at Easter, it would not be a bad idea to sprinkle the wafers with that drug which was used to bring the Emperor Henry VII to justice. It may perhaps be objected that this proceeding carries an inherent risk, in that we might administer the rat-poison to the Molinists as well. It is not a flippant point. But no plan is without its drawbacks, and no system but threatens ruin at some point or other. If we allowed ourselves to be hindered by every little difficulty, we should never see anything through to the end. And besides, since the purpose is to secure the greatest possible good, we must not throw our arms up in horror if this ultimate good brings in its wake a few unpleasant consequences which are of no great importance.

We have nothing to reproach ourselves with. It is proven that all the so-called Reformers and Jansenists are married to Hell; we are doing no more than hasten their honeymoon a little.

It is equally evident that Paradise belongs by right to the Molinists. Therefore, in killing them by mistake, with no evil intention, we shall accelerate their entry into heavenly bliss. In both cases, we are the agents of Providence.

As for those who might be somewhat shocked by the numbers involved, Your Reverence might remind them that, from the first flourishing days of the Church up till 1707, that is for about fourteen hundred years, theology has been responsible for the massacre of more than fifty million human beings, and that I propose to strangle, or eviscerate, or poison, only about six and a half million.

It might be further objected that my mathematics are faulty and that I have violated the rules of just proportion; for they will say that if in fourteen centuries only fifty million men have perished for nice distinctions and theological formulas, that makes an annual total of thirty-five thousand seven hundred and fourteen individuals (plus a fraction), and that my proposals would kill six million sixty-four thousand two hundred and eighty-five (with fraction) above the allowance for this year. That kind of quibbling is, in truth, very childish; it is even impious. For is it not obvious that my policy will save the life of every good Catholic until the end of time? One would never get anything done if one had to respond to every frivolous objection.

I am, with greatest respect, most Reverend Father,
Your humble and devoted and compassionate R.,[169]
Native of Angoulême, Prefect of the Congregation.

The plan was never put into execution, because Le Tellier found it a trifle awkward, and besides the reverend father was sent into exile the following year. But as one ought to look at both sides of any question, it is right to investigate whether there be some cases where one might properly accept, at least in part, the views of Father Le Tellier's correspondent. It seems that it would be difficult to execute the plan in all its details. But we should examine the circumstances in which it would be correct to break on the wheel, hang by the neck, or throw into a galley, those people who do not share our opinions; such is the purpose of the next chapter.

[169] Ravaillac.

18

The only cases in which intolerance conforms to human laws

In order that a government should not arrogate the right to punish man's mistakes, it is necessary that these mistakes should not be seen as criminal. They only become criminal when they threaten to undermine society, and they undermine society whenever they inspire fanaticism. Therefore, to be entitled to society's toleration, men should start by renouncing fanaticism.

If a band of young Jesuits, knowing that the Church holds reprobates in horror, knowing also that the Jansenists have been condemned by papal bull and are therefore reprobates, then go off and set fire to a house belonging to the fathers of the Oratory because one of their number, Father Quesnel,[170] was a Jansenist, it is clear that the government would be obliged to punish those Jesuits.

Similarly, if they have promulgated criminal doctrines, and if their institution is operated contrary to the laws of the land, then there is nothing for it but to dissolve their society, abolish the order of Jesuits and return its members to ordinary citizenship; which they may imagine to be a disaster, but which, in reality, does them a power of good. For what is wrong with wearing a short coat instead of a cassock, or with being free instead of a slave? In peacetime, whole regiments are disbanded without complaint; why should the Jesuits make such a fuss when they are disbanded for the sake of peace?

Should the Franciscans, in an access of zealous loyalty to the Virgin Mary, take it into their heads to pull down the Dominicans' church because these latter

---

[170] Pasquier Quesnel (1634–1719), one of the most prominent Jansenists largely by virtue of his book *Réflexions morales sur le Nouveau Testament*, which set out the Jansenist position more eloquently than any other apology. The papal bull *Unigenitus* identified 101 sentences from this book as heretical.

believe that Mary was born with original sin, then they would have to expect the same kind of treatment as was meted out to the Jesuits.

One could say as much for the Lutherans and Calvinists. It is no use their protesting, 'We follow the dictates of our consciences; better to obey God than man; we represent the genuine flock; we have a duty to exterminate the wolves', for it is evident from such language that they are themselves the wolves.

One of the most astonishing instances of fanaticism concerned a tiny Danish sect which had been founded upon the best principle in the world; for these enthusiasts wanted no less than to secure eternal salvation for their fellow men. However, there flowed from this ideal the most singular consequences. Armed with the knowledge that all infants who die unbaptised go to Hell, and that those who have the good fortune to die immediately after having been baptised enjoy eternal bliss, they set about the slaughter of every newly baptised little boy and girl they could lay their hands on. No doubt they thereby bestowed upon them the finest blessing it was possible to imagine – simultaneous protection from sin, from the miseries of earthly existence, and from Hell-fire, as well as a guaranteed place in Heaven. But these kind folk did not pause to reflect that it is forbidden to commit a small evil in order to provoke a greater good; nor that they had no rights of disposal over the lives of these little children; nor that most parents are weak enough to prefer having their children near them than to see their throats cut in readiness for Paradise; nor, in short, that magistrates are obliged to punish murder, even when committed with the best intentions.

The Jews appear to have more right than anyone to rob and murder us. Though there are a hundred examples of toleration in the Old Testament, there are also some instances of severity sanctioned by law. God occasionally ordered them to kill all idolators, sparing only marriageable girls; they look upon us as idolaters; and though we are tolerant towards them these days, they could easily, if they got the upper hand, denude the world of all but our marriageable daughters.

Above all, they are under an inalienable duty to murder the whole Turkish race. This they could achieve with a clear conscience, for the Turks of today occupy the land of the Hittites, the Jebusites, the Amorites, Hivites, Samarians and so on, all peoples that were laid under a curse. Their various countries, covering an area of more than twenty-five leagues, were given to the Jews by several consecutive treaties. They therefore have the right to claim land which is theirs, and which the Muslims usurped more than a thousand years ago.

If the Jews were to argue along these lines today, it is clear that the only valid response would be summary execution.

These are about the only cases in which intolerance may be sanctioned by reason.

19
Account of a controversial dispute which happened in China

In the first years of the great Emperor Cam Hi's reign, a Mandarin of Canton one day heard from within his house a huge racket coming from the house next door, and was so alarmed that he enquired whether somebody was not being killed there. He was told that a Danish almoner, a Dutch chaplain and a Jesuit were engaged in argument. Thereupon, the Mandarin invited them into his home, gave them tea and sweetmeats, and asked them why they were quarrelling.

The Jesuit explained that it was painful for him, since he was always right, to have to deal with people who were always wrong. He had begun by making his points with the greatest restraint, but in the end his patience was exhausted.

The Mandarin made them all understand, in the gentlest possible way, that good manners were of paramount importance in any difference of opinion, and that in China nobody grew angry in dispute. He asked them what was the subject of their discussion.

'My lord', said the Jesuit, 'you shall judge of this matter. These two gentlemen refuse to submit to the decisions of the Council of Trent.'[171]

'I am surprised', said the Mandarin, and turning to the others, told them, 'It seems to me, my good sirs, that you should respect the opinions expressed by a great assembly. I do not know what the Council of Trent is, but it is obvious that several persons thinking together are likely to be better informed than one

---

[171] The Council of Trent (1545–63) was one of the most important councils in the history of the Roman Catholic Church. Summoned to combat the threat from Protestant movements, it affirmed the knowledge gleaned from medieval scholasticism, enlarged the creed, organised the clergy, and made the position of the Pope unassailable.

person reflecting alone. No one must believe that he knows better than anyone else, or that the power of understanding resides in his head alone. So teaches our great Confucius. If you take my advice, you will do well to reconcile yourselves with the Council of Trent.'

Then it was the Dane's turn to have a word. 'His lordship speaks with the greatest wisdom', he said. 'We respect great assemblies as we should. Indeed, we are entirely in agreement with several assemblies which took place before that of Trent.'

'Ah', said the Mandarin, 'if that's the case, then I do beg your pardon. You may well be right. In other words, you and the Dutchman are in complete agreement against this poor Jesuit?'

'Not at all', interjected the Dutchman. 'This Dane entertains opinions almost as extravagant as those of the Jesuit who played so sweet and reasonable with you. I cannot contain myself any longer!'

'I can't make you out', said the Mandarin. 'Are you not all three Christians? Haven't all three of you come into our empire to preach Christianity? Shouldn't you therefore have identical doctrines?'

'You see, my lord', said the Jesuit, 'these two people are mortal enemies to each other, and both are in dispute with me. It is therefore obvious that they must both be wrong, and that only I am right.'

'It is not obvious at all', replied the Mandarin. 'It is equally possible that all three of you are wrong. I should be curious to hear you expound your arguments one after the other.'

So the Jesuit delivered quite a long speech, during which the Dane and the Dutchman shrugged their shoulders, and the Mandarin understood not a word. Then the Dane took the floor, while his two adversaries looked upon him with contempt, and the Mandarin was none the wiser. The Dutchman did not fare any better in his turn. Finally, they all spoke at the same time and hurled gross insults at one another. The good Mandarin had the greatest difficulty in silencing them, upon which he said, 'If you want us to tolerate your teaching in this country, you must start by being neither intolerant nor intolerable yourselves.'

When he left the house the Jesuit encountered a Dominican missionary, and told him that he had carried his argument, because truth always triumphs. 'If I had been there, you would not have prevailed', replied the Dominican. 'I would have shown you to be a liar and idolator.' The quarrel then grew hot; the Dominican and the Jesuit fell to fighting and seized each other by the hair. When the Mandarin heard of this scandalous conduct he sent them both to prison. A deputy Mandarin asked the judge:

'How long does Your Excellency require that they should remain incarcerated?'

'Until they come to agreement', said the judge.

'Ah', said the deputy, 'in that case they will be in prison for the rest of their lives.'

'All right', said the judge. 'Let's say until they forgive each other.'

'They will never forgive', said the other. 'I know them.'

'Well, then', said the judge, 'until they *pretend* to forgive each other.'

20
Whether it is useful to hold the people in superstition

Such is the weakness of the human race, and such their perversity, that they would doubtless prefer to be subject to every conceivable superstition, provided it was not murderous, than to live without religion. Mankind has always been in need of a restraining influence, and however ridiculous it might be to make sacrifice to fauns, elves and water-nymphs, it was certainly both more reasonable and more serviceable to worship these fantastic images of the deity than to give oneself over to Atheism. A committed, violent and powerful Atheist would be as pernicious a scourge as the most bloodthirsty religious bigot.

When men are bereft of sane ideas about divinity, false notions take their place, just as in times of economic depression counterfeit money circulates because reliable money is scarce. The pagan was deterred from committing crime for fear of punishment from his false gods. In like manner, the Malabar[172] cringes before his pagod. Wherever a community has taken root, religion is essential; while laws are established to place a curb upon open crimes, religion deals with private ones.

But once men have reached the stage where they can embrace a true and holy religion, superstitions become not only superfluous, but downright dangerous. One does not feed on acorns those to whom God has given bread.

Superstition is to religion what astrology is to astronomy, that is the very foolish daughter of a wise and intelligent mother. These two daughters have long held the entire world in subjection.

When in the Dark Ages one was hard put to it to find even two feudal lords

---

[172] Malabar is a district on the west coast of India, by Madras. Voltaire, by referring to 'the Malabar', presumably means to encompass the Hindu in general.

who might possess a copy of the New Testament, it was perfectly excusable to use fables by way of explanation to the uneducated, which included of course those very feudal lords, their cretinous wives and their brutish vassals. They were asked to believe that St Christopher carried the child Jesus across a river on his shoulders;[173] they were fed on stories of witchcraft and possession; it was easy for them to conceive that St Genou could cure the gout and St Clare cured sore eyes.[174] Children believed in the bogeyman and their fathers in St Francis's girdle. There abounded a positively infinite number of relics.

The rust from so many superstitions continued to infect the people, even after religion became less cluttered and more pure. When M. de Noailles, Bishop of Châlons,[175] removed the so-called relic of Christ's sacred navel and threw it on the fire, the whole town of Châlons rose up to prosecute him; but the bishop was endowed with courage as well as piety, and before long he convinced the townfolk that one could worship Jesus in spirit and in truth without the necessity of having his navel placed in a church.

Those whom we call Jansenists contributed in no small way towards the gradual eradication from the national consciousness of false notions which dishonour the Christian religion. People no longer believe that it is enough to recite a prayer to the Virgin Mary for thirty days in order to have everything they want out of life and to be able to sin with impunity.

The common people began finally to suspect that it was not St Genevieve who gave or withheld rain,[176] but that God Himself was in control of His elements. The monks were dumbfounded that their saints no longer performed miracles; and if the authors of the life of St Francis Xavier were to come back to earth, they would not now have the temerity to write that he resurrected nine corpses, that he could be on water and on land at one and the

---

[173] *Christophoros* in Greek signifies 'he who carries Christ', i.e. carries the spirit of Christ in his heart. The leap to the physical manifestation of a strong man offering a piggy-back to the child Jesus is entire invention, and the character and deeds of the original man, if he existed, are lost. Legend says he was a Canaanite of great strength, whose real name might have been Reprobus.

[174] St Genou or Genulphe is a legendary martyr, said to have lived in Rome in the third century and to have gone from there to Berry in France.

St Clare of Assisi (1194–1253) was a disciple of St Francis, a noblewoman who refused two offers of marriage to devote herself to the spiritual life. Francis set her up with her sister St Agnes in a house in Assisi which became the nucleus of an order variously known as Minoresses, Poor Ladies or Poor Clares.

[175] Louis-Antoine de Noailles (1651–1729), Bishop of Cahors in 1679, of Châlons-sur-Marne in 1680, Archbishop of Paris in 1695 and cardinal in 1699. In the protracted dispute between Jansenists and Jesuits, Cardinal de Noailles was a firm supporter of Quesnel and the Jansenists of Port-Royal, and consequently hostile to the papal bull *Unigenitus*.

[176] St Genevieve is venerated as the Patroness of Paris. Her prayers deflected Attila the Hun, and her relics have been known to dissolve epidemics. She lived from about 420 to 500.

same time, and that when he lost his crucifix at sea, it was returned to him by a crab.[177]

The same with excommunication. Our historians have told us that when King Robert was excommunicated by Pope Gregory V for having married his god-mother, Princess Bertha,[178] his domestics threw the food they had served him out of the window, and Queen Bertha was brought to bed of a goose as a punishment for incest. Nowadays we are permitted to doubt whether the pages of a king of France would chuck his dinner into the street because His Majesty had been excommunicated, or that the Queen, for similar offences, would give birth to a gosling.

Should there be a convulsionary still lurking in some dark corner of the suburbs, we would have to tell him that he suffers from a disease transmitted by lice which attack only the dregs of the population. With each day that passes, the power of reason is seeping as much into the houses of tradesmen as into the grand mansions of the nobility. We must needs harvest the fruits of this reason, particularly since it is impossible to prevent their blossoming. Now that France has been enlightened by Pascal, by Nicole, by Arnauld, by Bossuet, Descartes and Gassendi, by Bayle, Fontenelle and the rest, she can no longer be governed quite as she was when the likes of Garasse and Menot held sway.[179]

If the masters of error, by which I mean the great masters who were for so long rewarded and honoured for having brutalised the human race, if today they were to require us to believe that seed must rot before it can sprout, that the earth sits solidly on its foundations and does not turn around the sun, that tides are not a natural effect of gravitation, that a rainbow is not formed by the refraction and reflection of light, and so on, and if they further called upon passages from Holy Scripture which they barely understand to prop up their ordinances, in what terms would they be regarded by educated people? Would 'blockheads' be too strong? And if these clever teachers used compulsion and the threat of persecution in order to make their insulting ignorance prevail, would 'tyrants' be misplaced?

The more contempt we pour upon the superstitions of monks, the greater is the respect due to bishops and their clergy; for these only do good, while the

---

[177] St Francis Xavier (1506–52), pioneer missionary to Goa and Japan, whose task was rendered the more difficult by the example offered by European settlers. His body is preserved at Goa.

[178] Robert II, King of the Franks, known as 'Robert the Pious' (c. 970–1031), was the son of Hugh Capet. He married three times, his second wife being Princess Bertha of Burgundy, a cousin also previously married. Robert had in fact been godfather to one of her children (not the other way round). Papal displeasure forced the couple to separate, although Robert continued to be friendly with Bertha after his third marriage.

[179] Father François Garasse (1585–1631) was a Jesuit noted for excessive passion in argument. Michel Menot (1440–1518) was a Franciscan friar nicknamed 'Golden Tongue' (*La Langue d'Or*) owing to his oratory.

superstitions of foreign monasteries have done very much harm. Yet of all superstitions is not the most dangerous that which demands we hate our neighbour on account of his opinion? Is it not evident that it would be far more in accordance with reason to worship the holy navel, the holy foreskin, the milk and the robe of the Virgin Mary, than to detest and to persecute one's fellow man?

21
Virtue is better than knowledge

The fewer dogmas one has to deal with, the fewer the disputes over them; and the fewer the disputes, the less the risk of calamity. If this is not true, then I am much mistaken.

Religion is instituted in order to make us happy in this life and in the next. What is necessary to be happy in the life to come? That we be just. And to be happy in *this* life, in so far as our perverse nature will allow, what is necessary? That we be tolerant and merciful.

It would be the height of folly to attempt to bring all men to think alike on matters of metaphysics. It would be much simpler to conquer the entire world by force of arms than to subdue and shackle the minds of a single town.

Euclid easily succeeded in convincing everyone of the truths of geometry. Why? Because there is not one which is not a demonstrable corollary of this little axiom: *two and two make four*. It is not quite the same when it comes to the subtleties of metaphysics and theology.

When Bishop Alexander and the priest Arius started arguing about the manner in which the Word emanated from God the Father, the Emperor Constantine wrote to them with these words, reported by both Eusebius and Socrates: *You are a couple of prize fools to argue over matters you cannot understand.*[180]

If the two contending parties had been wise enough to recognise that the

---

[180] Constantine's letter, preserved by Eusebius, is amusingly paraphrased by Voltaire. The Emperor wrote to the squabbling parties (arguing over the Arian heresy, later to be condemned by the Council of Nicaea; see note 95 above) tactfully suggesting that Alexander and Arius were both right in substance and equally wrong to bring to public notice arguments which would only confuse an ignorant populace.

Emperor was right, the Christian world would have been spared three centuries of bloodshed.

Indeed, what could be more stupid or dreadful than to address mankind thus: 'My friends, it is not sufficient that you be faithful subjects, dutiful children, compassionate parents, honest neighbours, that you practise all the virtues, cultivate friendship, are never ungrateful, and worship Jesus Christ in peace. You must also know how it is to be begotten from all eternity without being made for all eternity. And if you cannot distinguish the homousian in the hypostasis,[181] we pronounce that you shall be boiled in Hell; and in the meantime, we shall start by cutting your throats'?

Had one presented such a proposition to Archimedes, or Posidonius, or Varro, or Cato, or Cicero, how, one wonders, would they have responded?

Constantine did not follow through his resolution to impose silence upon the two disputants. He could have summoned these champion hair-splitters to his palace; he could have asked them by what authority they disturbed the world; he could have said, 'Do you hold exclusive title to the divine family? What does it matter to you that the Word be engendered or made, provided we serve it faithfully, provided we preach good moral values and practise them as best we can? I have done many things wrong in my life, and so have you; you are ambitious, and so am I; it has cost me some swindling and some cruelty to attain the empire; I have murdered nearly all those near to me, and I am now sorry for it; I desire to expiate my crimes by bringing tranquillity to the Roman Empire; do not prevent me from doing the only good action which may enable my past iniquities to be forgotten; help me end my days in peace.' Perhaps he would have gained nothing by this speech. Perhaps on the contrary it flattered him to preside over a council, in a long red cloak and his head loaded with diamonds.

That, however, is what opened the door to all the scourges from Asia which were later unleashed upon the western world. Each hot dispute over a text of Scripture gave birth to furious rage, armed with sophistical argument in one hand and a dagger in the other, which plunged the whole of civilised mankind into madness and cruelty. Those who came afterwards – the Huns, the Heruli, the Goths and the Vandals – did infinitely less harm; indeed, their greatest crime was eventually to join in these fatal squabbles.

[181] This refers to the arguments about consubstantiality. (See note 93 above and note 184 below.)

22

On universal tolerance

It requires no great skill in argument or gift of eloquence to prove that Christians should tolerate one another. I will go further: I tell you, we ought to regard every man as our brother. What? The Turk, my brother? The Chinaman, my brother? The Jew and the Siamese as well? Yes, assuredly, for are we not all children of the same Father and creatures of the same God?

But these people despise us, they call us idolators! Very well, I shall tell them they are very much mistaken. It seems to me that I could perhaps shake the arrogant stubbornness of an imam or a Buddhist monk if I were to speak to them more or less in this vein:

'This little globe, which is really only a spot, rolls in space along with so many other globes, all part of this immensity in which we are all lost. The human being, roughly five feet high, is patently of very little consequence in the vast Creation. One of these tiny creatures says to some other of his species, in Arabia or Asia it might be, "Now listen to me, for the God of all these worlds has shown me the truth; there are nine hundred million little ants like us on this earth, but God cherishes only my ant-hill and absolutely loathes all the others to all eternity; so mine will be the only happy ant-hill, and all the rest will be miserable for ever and ever."' The others will then stop me and ask, 'Who is this idiot who talks such nonsense?' And I shall be obliged to reply, 'It is yourselves.' I shall then attempt to calm them down, but it will not be easy.

Next, I shall address myself to the Christians, and I would venture to speak to a Dominican, for example, one appointed a judge of the Inquisition, as follows: 'My brother, you know that each province of Italy boasts its own dialect, and that people do not talk in Venice or Bergamo at all as they do in Florence. The

Academy of Crusca[182] has fixed the standards of the language; its Dictionary establishes a rule from which one departs at one's peril, and Buonmattei's *Grammar*[183] is an infallible guide to be followed at all times; but do you think the President of the Academy or, in his absence, Buonmattei could in all conscience have cut out the tongues of those Venetians and Bergamese who continued to talk in their own *patois?*'

The Inquisitor might reply: 'That is not the same thing at all; we are talking about the salvation of your soul; it is for your own good that the Director of the Inquisition commands you to be arrested on the statement of a single person, be he the most infamous rogue; it is for your own good that you should have no lawyer to defend you and that even the name of your accuser should be kept from you; it is for your own good that the Inquisitor promises mercy and delivers the death sentence, that he sends you off to be tortured in five different ways, that you are finally flogged or sent to the galleys or burnt alive in ceremonial fashion; Father Ivonet, Doctors Chucalon, Zanchinus, and half a dozen others, are all adamant on the point, and this holy practice will admit of no contradiction.'

I should then take the liberty of answering him thus: 'Perhaps, my brother, you are right; I am persuaded of all the benefits you wish to bestow upon me, but could I not be saved without going through all that?'

It is true that absurd horrors like these do not deform the face of the earth every day, but they have happened often enough that one might easily compile a volume much larger than the gospels which condemn them. Not only is it very cruel, in this short life, to persecute those who do not think as we do, but I suspect it is also very bold indeed to pronounce their eternal damnation. It seems to me that it hardly belongs to such transient atoms as we are to usurp the decrees of the Creator. I am a long way from wishing to contradict the maxim that *There is no salvation outside the Church.* I respect it, as I respect all its teaching. But, in truth, do we know all the ways of God and the full extent of His mercy? Is it not permitted we should hope in Him as much as fear Him? Is it not sufficient to be faithful servants of the Church? Must each one of us presume to take upon himself the authority of God and decide, in His place, upon the eternal fate of our fellow men?

When we wear mourning for the King of Sweden, or Denmark, or England, or Prussia, do we tell ourselves that we are in mourning for a reprobate who will burn in Hell for all time? There are forty million people in Europe who do not belong to the Church of Rome; are we to tell each of them: 'Sir, since you are

[182] L'Accademia della Crusca was founded in Florence in 1582 and produced a standard dictionary of the Italian language in 1612.
[183] Benedetto Buonmattei (1581–1648), Florentine philologist who began by studying mathematics and applied the same scientific methods to his study of grammar. He taught at Padua, wrote a book on Dante, and was famous eventually for his analysis of the Tuscan language.

irrevocably damned, I cannot eat with you, talk to you, or have anything to do with you whatever'?

Can one imagine an ambassador of France secretly muttering to himself, as he presents his credentials to the Grand Ruler of Turkey, 'His Highness will undoubtedly burn in eternal Hell-fire because he allowed himself to be circumcised'? If he really believed that the ruler was a mortal enemy of God and the object of divine retribution, could he so much as talk to him? Perhaps he should not even be sent as envoy to such a person. With whom then are we to deal? Is there any duty of political life which we could properly undertake if we genuinely thought we were having truck with souls damned to eternity?

All ye manifold worshippers of a merciful God! If you are hard of heart, if in adoring Him whose entire law is contained in the words *Love thy God and thy neighbour* you have smothered that pure and holy doctrine with sophistries and unfathomable controversies; if you have provoked bitter argument over a new word, or even sometimes a single letter of the alphabet;[184] if you have sought to bring eternal punishment to bear for the omission of a few phrases or details of ceremony which other peoples could not possibly be aware of; then, through my tears and lamentation for the fate of humankind, I must say to you:

'Come with me to the Day of Judgement, when God will give unto every man according to his deeds. I there envisage all the dead of all the ages, and of our own, appearing before the Almighty. Are you absolutely sure that our Creator and Father in Heaven will say to the wise and virtuous Confucius, to Solon the law-giver, to Pythagoras, Zaleucus, Socrates and Plato, to the divine Antoninus, to the good Trajan and Titus, that adornment of the human race, to Epictetus and so many other models among mankind, "Go, you monsters! Go and suffer torments of infinite intensity and duration; your punishment will continue for ever and ever! As for you others who are so dear to me – Jean Châtel, Ravaillac, Damiens, Cartouche and the rest – you who died according to the correct formula, stay at my right hand and partake of my kingdom and my happiness in eternity"?'

You will recoil in horror at these words, and indeed, once they have escaped my pen, I have nothing further to add.

---

[184] Voltaire refers to two warring sects, the Homoiousions and Homoousions, who were active during the reign of Constantine.

23
A prayer to God

It is not now to mankind that I address myself, but to thee, God of all beings, of all worlds, and of all ages, if it be permitted to feeble creatures lost in the immensity of space and imperceptible to the rest of the universe to presume to ask Thee aught, Thou who hast given all and whose secrets are as immutable as they are eternal. Deign to look with pity upon those errors which are inherent in our nature, that these errors be not our downfall! Thou didst not give us a heart in order that we should hate one another, nor hands to kill each other with; grant that we may help one another to bear the burden of a difficult and transient life! Let not the trifling differences between the clothes which cover our weak bodies, between our inadequate languages, between our ridiculous customs, our imperfect laws and our insane opinions, between our various conditions, so disproportionate in our eyes and so equal in Thine; let not these little nuances which distinguish the atoms known as men give excuse for hatred or persecution! Grant that those who light candles in the full light of day to worship Thee should look with kindness upon those others who are content with the light of Thy sun! That those who cover their garment with a white veil in order to declare that they love Thee should not detest those others who say the same thing beneath a cloak of black wool! That it should be accounted as good to adore Thee in a jargon derived from some ancient tongue as in a more modern jargon! That those whose garments are dyed red or purple and who lord it over a scrap of a tiny patch of the mud of this world, and who own a few round-shaped objects made of a certain metal, should enjoy what they are pleased to call their status and their riches without pride, and that the rest should observe them without envy; for Thou knowest there is nought to be envied in these little vanities, and nought to be proud of.

May all men remember they are brothers! May they abhor the tyranny which would imprison the soul just as much as they execrate that highway robbery which makes off with the fruit of honest work and application. If the scourges of war are not to be avoided, let us at least not hate one another or tear each other apart in the midst of peace, but let us use the moment of our earthly existence to praise, in a thousand different but equal languages, from Siam to California, Thy goodness which has given us that moment.

24
Post-scriptum

While I was writing this treatise, with the sole desire of making mankind more compassionate and charitable, another author was employed in writing with an entirely contrary purpose; for everyone has his own way of thinking. This gentleman[185] has published a little code of persecution entitled *The Harmony of Religion and Humanity* (for which please read *Inhumanity*; it must be a printer's error).

The author of this pious libel takes as his authority St Augustine, who, having once preached charity and benevolence, then turned to advocate persecution. Remark that by then he was in a position of some power, besides which he was apt to change his mind frequently. This author also cites Bossuet, the Bishop of Meaux, who harried the celebrated Fénelon, Archbishop of Cambrai, for having dared to state in print that God was worth loving for His own sake.

I gladly admit that Bossuet was a man gifted with eloquence. Likewise, I am happy to allow that Augustine, Bishop of Hippo, though logical thought was not always his strong point, was much more fluent than the rest of the Africans. But I permit myself the liberty of quoting Armande in *Les Femmes savantes* to the effect that

> *If others our examples we must make,*
> *We should their virtues not their failings take.*[186]

To the Bishop of Hippo I would say, 'Monseigneur, you have changed your opinion. Allow me to adhere to your earlier point of view, which, in truth, I

---

[185] L'abbé Malvaux, whose book was published in 1762, the year before Voltaire's *Treatise*.
[186]   '*Quand sur une personne on prétend se régler,*
         C'est par les beaux côtés qu'il lui faut ressembler.'
         (Molière, *Les Femmes savantes*, Act I, Sc. 1)

think the better one.' And I would say to the Bishop of Meaux, 'Monseigneur, you are a great man. I consider you to be at least as learned as St Augustine, and far his superior in eloquence. But why must you so torment your colleague, who was just as eloquent as you in his way, and much more likeable?'

The author of our holy libel on inhumanity is neither a Bossuet nor a St Augustine; it seems to me he is excellently cut out to be an Inquisitor, and I dearly wish he had been at the head of that fine tribunal in Goa. Moreover he is obviously a statesman, to judge by the grand political principles he sets forth. 'If you should find among you many dissidents', he writes, 'handle them gently, use persuasion upon them. But if they be few in number, you will find the gallows or the galleys to be highly effective.' Such is the advice he offers on pages 89 and 90.

Thank God I am a good Catholic, and have nothing to fear from what the Huguenots call martyrdom; but if this person ever becomes Prime Minister, as he seems to flatter himself he might, I give notice that I shall leave for England the day he receives his letters patent.

In the meantime, I can only thank Heaven for making sure that people of his kind are always deficient in reason. He goes so far as to count Bayle[187] among the supporters of intolerance; how very clever and perceptive; and because Bayle agrees that rogues and trouble-makers should be punished, our author concludes from this that one must persecute with fire and sword people of good faith who live in peace (p. 98).

Virtually the whole of his book is an imitation of the *Apology for the Massacre of St Bartholomew*. You hear the voice of either this apologist or his echo; in both cases, one must hope that neither the master nor his pupil will ever take part in the government of the State.

But if it ever happens that they should reach positions of power, I make them a petition in advance, concerning two lines on page 93 of the said pious lampoon: 'Is it right to sacrifice the welfare of the entire nation in order to protect that of a mere twentieth part of it?'

Let us suppose for a moment that there are indeed in France twenty Roman Catholics for every one Huguenot; I am not about to suggest the single Huguenot should gobble up the twenty Catholics; but, conversely, on what grounds should those twenty Catholics devour the lonely Huguenot? And why should the Huguenot be prevented from marrying? Are there not bishops, abbots and monks aplenty whose estates lie in Dauphiné, Gévaudan, by Agde and Carcassonne? These bishops, abbots and monks, do they not count amongst those who work their estates several farmers who have the misfortune not to believe the doctrine of transubstantiation? Is it not in the interest of the bishops, abbots and monks, and of the public at large, that these farmers

---

[187] Pierre Bayle (1647–1706), author of *Dictionnaire historique*, the bold scepticism and liberal independence of which made him the precursor of Voltaire and the *encyclopédistes*.

should have large families? Are those who take communion only in one form to be alone permitted to have children?[188] In very truth, that is neither fair nor honest.

'The revocation of the Edict of Nantes did not cause as much inconvenience as has been claimed', says our author.

If anyone does attribute more mischief to the revocation than it in fact produced, then he exaggerates; and almost all historians do tend to exaggerate as a matter of course. But equally at fault are these polemicists who make light of the evils that are legitimately laid at their door. We should not rely for the truth upon either the professors of Paris or the preachers of Amsterdam.

Let us take as arbiter the Count of Avaux, Ambassador to Holland from 1685 to 1688. He says in his memoirs (Vol. v, p. 181) that one man offered to reveal the whereabouts of more than twenty million livres which the persecuted Huguenots contrived to spirit out of France. Louis XIV replied to M. d'Avaux: 'The information I receive every day telling of an infinite number of conversions leaves no further room for doubt that even the most pigheaded will eventually follow the rest.'

One may see from this letter that Louis XIV had a very high opinion of the scope of his power. Every morning he was accustomed to being told, 'Sire, you are the greatest monarch on earth; the whole world will be proud to think like you, as soon as they have heard a pronouncement from your lips.' Pellisson, who made a fortune as first clerk in the Treasury and had spent three years in the Bastille as an accomplice with Fouquet; Pellisson, who started as a Calvinist and ended a deacon and a beneficed priest, who published prayers destined for the mass and the sonnets destined for Iris, who had secured for himself the posts of treasurer and official converter of heretics; this Pellisson turned up every three months with a long list of recantations purchased at seven or eight écus apiece, and had his sovereign believe that he could convert the entire Turkish nation for the same price whenever he wanted. Courtiers took it in turns to deceive the King; is there any wonder he was seduced?

This same M. d'Avaux, on the other hand, sent a despatch to his king indicating that a certain Vincent employed more than five hundred labourers in the vicinity of Angoulême and that if he were to quit the kingdom it would occasion much hardship (Vol. v, p. 194).

Again, he gave information that the Prince of Orange had already raised two regiments of refugee French officers, and the crews of three French ships had

---

[188] This refers to the disputes whether the laity should receive communion in both forms (bread and wine) or in one form only. Until the eleventh century communion was always in both forms, but then in 1099 Pope Paschal II issued a decree which permitted children to omit the wine and invalids the bread. The Councils of Constance (1415) and Trent (1545–63) approved communion under a single form, and communion using bread and wine was discontinued in the Catholic Church.

deserted to the prince's side. There was, besides, a company of refugee cadets under the command of two captains (p. 240). Finally, this ambassador wrote on 9 May 1686 to M. de Seignelay that he 'cannot disguise his concern at seeing French manufacturing business establish itself in Holland, whence it will never again emerge'.

Add to this evidence the testimony of the many intendants of the kingdom during the year 1698, and then judge whether the revocation of the Edict of Nantes has not done more harm than good, notwithstanding the opinion of the estimable author of *The Harmony of Religion and Inhumanity*.

A Marshal of France, known for his superior intellect, a few years ago made the following shrewd observation: 'I do not know if the custom of dragooning was ever necessary, but I do know that it is now necessary it should cease.'

I confess that I went perhaps a little too far in publishing the letter from Father Le Tellier's correspondent in which the good priest recommended the use of gunpowder. I told myself that nobody would believe me, or that people would think the letter a forgery. I was able fortunately to abandon the vestiges of scruple when I read on page 149 of *The Harmony of Religion and Inhumanity* these comforting words: 'The total extermination of all Protestants in the country would not weaken France any more than the practice of letting blood weakens a patient of sound constitution.'

So the compassionate minister of Christ who informed us a little while ago that Protestants composed one-twentieth of the nation is happy to spill the blood of this one-twentieth in an operation which he apparently compares to a phlebotomical evacuation. May God preserve us and him alike from the other three-twentieths!

Since therefore this worthy man has proposed murdering one-twentieth of the nation, what is there to inhibit Father Le Tellier's friend from advocating that we poison, slaughter and blow to smithereens one-third? Given which, it is highly probable that the letter to Le Tellier is genuine.

Our saintly author concludes with the conviction that intolerance is an excellent thing, 'because it was never expressly condemned by Jesus Christ'. But neither did Christ condemn those who would happily set the whole of Paris ablaze; is that sufficient reason to canonise arsonists?

Thus it happens that wherever the gentle and benevolent voice of Nature is heard, Fanaticism, the sworn enemy of Nature, is also heard to howl in protest. And whenever peace is offered to mankind, Intolerance arms herself to the teeth to oppose it. May the international arbiters who have given peace to Europe now decide which is to be preferred, the spirit of peace and harmony on one side, or the spirit of discord and hatred on the other.

25
Sequel and conclusion

On 7 March 1763 a Council of State was held at Versailles, at which were present all the ministers of the government, with the Chancellor presiding, to hear the report of Monsieur de Crosne, the Master of Requests, on the Calas affair. He gave his account with the impartiality of a judge, the precision of a man acquainted with all the details of the case, and the straightforward, honest eloquence of an orator and statesman, as alone befitted such an assembly. An enormous throng of people of all ranks awaited the decision of the Council in the Long Gallery of the palace. In a short time the King was informed that the Council had come to a unanimous resolution: that the Parliament of Toulouse be ordered to send forthwith to the Council all papers relative to the trial and all considered reasons for the verdict which sent Calas to death on the wheel; His Majesty approved the decision of the Council.

So justice and humanity do still reside in the breasts of men! and more particularly in the Council of a deservedly loved monarch. The concerns of an unhappy family of humble citizens have been considered by His Majesty, his ministers, the Chancellor and the entire Council, with as much careful scrutiny as they would devote to the greatest affairs of State such as war and peace. The judges have been guided by a love of equity and the interests of their fellow human beings. Thanks be to the God of mercy, source of all justice and virtue!

We should point out that we have never met the unfortunate Calas whom eight Toulousain judges sent to his death on the flimsiest evidence, in contravention of both the ordinances of our reigning monarchs and international law. Nor do we have acquaintance with his son Marc-Antoine, the strange manner of whose death caused the judges to fall into error, nor the respectable and unhappy mother, nor her innocent daughters who have travelled two hundred leagues with her to place their ordeal and their honesty at their sovereign's feet.

God Almighty knows that, in setting down our views about tolerance on the occasion of the murder of Jean Calas by the spirit of intolerance, we have been solely motivated by a desire for justice, truth and peace.

We intended no offence against the eight judges of Toulouse by pointing out that they had made a mistake, as the entire Council of State now seems to agree; on the contrary, we have opened to them an opportunity to excuse themselves before the whole of Europe. This they can do by confessing that their judgement was misled by false evidence and the hysteria of a crazed mob; by asking the widow's forgiveness; and by making amends, as far as is in their power, for the ruin of an innocent family and joining those who would now help and succour them in their distress. Since it is they who have caused the unjust death of the father, it is to them that the children should look for a father's care, always supposing that the orphans could bring themselves to accept from their hands an inadequate token of the most righteous repentance. It would be good for the judges to make such an offer, and for the family politely to decline it.

In particular, it behoves Sieur David, *Capitoul* of Toulouse, being the first instigator of this persecution, to give the first example of remorse. He insulted the father as he lay dying on the scaffold. That was a display of the most outrageous cruelty. But since God forgives, it is also the duty of men to forgive those who make proper atonement for their offences.

I have received the following letter from Languedoc, dated 20 February 1763:

> Your book on the subject of tolerance strikes me as full of humanity and truth, but I am afraid it may do more harm than good to the Calas family. It could well antagonise the eight judges who gave sentence of death. They will ask parliament to have your book burnt. And the bigots, who will not disappear, will respond with ferocious energy against the voice of reason ... [etc.]

This is my reply:

The judges of Toulouse may have my book burnt if they so desire. Nothing could be easier. After all, the *Lettres provinciales*[189] were burnt, and they were

---

[189] The eighteen *Lettres provinciales* of Blaise Pascal were published anonymously between 23 January 1656 and 24 March 1657 and caused an immediate sensation. Pascal wrote with passionate eloquence, irony and even humour in defence of the Jansenist position, which had been under constant attack from the Jesuits, the Molinists and the Vatican. Pascal had to change his name and address frequently during the months of publication to avoid detection or arrest, and the *Lettres provinciales* were placed on the prohibited index by the Vatican. He afterwards intended to write an Apology for Christianity, of which we have only the fragmented *Pensées* (1669–70).

doubtless of greater worth. Every man has the right to burn in his own house whatever books or papers are displeasing to him.

My book can do neither harm nor good to the Calas family, who are utterly unknown to me personally. The steadfast and impartial King's Council makes its judgement according to law, equity, the rules of evidence and due procedure, and cannot be influenced by a book which is in no way juridical and the subject of which has nothing whatever to do with the affair under review. It would be a waste of time, in this matter, to publish any number of tracts for or against the eight judges of Toulouse, for or against religious tolerance; neither the Council nor any other court of law would admit such books in evidence.

This essay on tolerance is a humble request made on behalf of humanity before the forces of power and discretion. I have tried to sow a seed from which one day there might be gathered a harvest. For the rest, we depend upon the fullness of time, the goodness of the King, the wisdom of his ministers, and the spirit of reason which is beginning to spread enlightenment everywhere.

Nature tells us all, 'You have been born weak and ignorant and are doomed to live out a few fleeting moments on earth before fertilising it with your corpses. Since you are weak, you must look after one another, and since you are ignorant you must educate each other. If the day comes that you are all of the same opinion (which is improbable, to say the least), and there remains one solitary man who clings to a different opinion, you must forgive him; for it is I who am responsible for making him think the way he does. I have given you strength with which to cultivate the ground and a flicker of intelligence to guide you. I have placed in each of your hearts a seed of compassion with which to help one another through life. Do not smother this seed; nor must you corrupt it; for it is divine. And do not substitute the pathetic squabbles of academic dispute for the voice of nature.

'I alone bind you still further one to another, despite yourselves, by your mutual needs even in the midst of those cruel wars of yours, waged on the slightest of pretexts, which provide an inexhaustible display of mistakes, mischances and misfortunes. I alone can put a stop to the disastrous consequences of those interminable divisions between the nobility and the judiciary, between both these two and the Church, between the urban dweller and the farmer, or the producer and consumer. None of them know the limits of their rights; but in the end, despite themselves, they will all listen to my voice as it speaks directly to their hearts. I alone preserve fairness in the law-courts where, without my intervention, everything would descend to caprice and vacillation, as men are confronted with a huge pile of laws, often framed haphazardly or to meet a transitory need, which differ from one province to another, from one town to another, and almost always contradict each other even within the same place. I alone can inspire true justice, whereas laws inspire naught but wrangling and subterfuge; he who listens to me will always reach the just decision, whereas he who looks only to reconcile contradictory views will go astray.

'There exists a very large building of which I laid the foundations with my own hands; it was solid and simple, and all men might enter it with safety; but they took it into their heads to add to it the most bizarre, useless and vulgar ornamentation, as a result of which the edifice is now falling into ruin on all sides and people pick up the stones and hurl them at one another's heads. To them I cry, "Stop! remove this disgusting debris which is all your work, and remain peacefully with me within the indestructible mansion of my creation."'[190]

[190] The 1763 edition of the *Treatise* ends here. The article which follows was added in 1765 in the second volume of the *Nouveaux Mélanges*.

Addendum: in which account is taken of the latest decision in favour of the Calas family

From 7 March 1763 until the final judgment, another two years were to pass. So easy is it for the forces of bigotry to snatch life from innocent persons, and so difficult for the powers of reason to oblige them to restore justice. Long periods of tedium, unavoidably associated with formal process, had to be endured. The less these formalities had been observed in the trial of Calas, the more important was it they should be rigorously applied by the Council of State. An entire twelvemonth was not long enough to force the Parliament of Toulouse to send all the documents to Paris, to examine them, and to report on them. M. de Crosne was once more entrusted with this burdensome undertaking. An assembly of nearly eighty judges quashed the verdict of Toulouse and ordered the trial to be reconsidered from scratch.

Other important matters at that time kept virtually all the courts of the kingdom busy. The Jesuits were being pursued, their communities abolished throughout France; they had been intolerant, and were now the victims of intolerance in their turn.

The extravagant language of statements of confession, of which they were believed to be the authors and were openly the publicists, had already brought the loathing of the country upon them. A huge bankruptcy incurred by one of their missionaries, which was thought to be partly fraudulent, finished them off. The mere juxtaposition of those words *missionary* and *bankrupt*, such unlikely bedfellows, served to condemn them in the hearts of men. Finally, the ruins of Port-Royal and the bones of so many famous men desecrated in their tombs and exhumed at the beginning of the century upon orders which could only have been given by the Jesuits, excited the nation's wrath against whatever little credit they had left. One may read the history of their proscription in an excellent book entitled *On the Destruction of the Jesuits in France*,[191] a scrupulously objective work, as one might expect from an author who is a philosopher, written with the exquisite style and eloquence of a Pascal, and moreover with a superior intelligence which is not blinded, as in Pascal, by those prejudices which occasionally afflict great men.

This mighty affair, which the Jesuits' supporters claimed was an affront to religion but most people regarded as her vindication, for several months so occupied public attention that the Calas trial was lost from view. But when the King assigned the final decision in the case to that tribunal called the Court of Requests,[192] this same public, which likes to jump from one drama to the next, immediately forgot the Jesuits and concentrated its whole gaze upon the Calas family.

The Court of Requests is a sovereign court composed of Masters of the Requests gathered to consider disputes between officers of the court, and also to rule upon whatever causes the King submits for its judgement. One could not choose a court better informed on the Calas affair, for these were precisely the same magistrates who had twice adjudicated on the preliminaries of the appeal, and who perfectly understood in all their particulars both the essence of the case and the manner in which it had been conducted. The widow of Jean Calas, his son, and M. Lavaisse all went back to prison. The old Catholic servant, who had not left her employers' side during the whole of that time when it was supposed, against all likelihood, that they were busy strangling their son, was brought up from the depths of Languedoc. The court sat to deliberate upon the identical evidence as had served to send Jean Calas to his death and his son Pierre into exile.

It was then that a fresh opinion by the eloquent M. de Beaumont was submitted, together with a statement from the young Lavaisse, so unjustly implicated in criminal proceedings by the Toulouse magistrates, who, to add insult to injury, had still failed to pronounce him innocent. This young man himself prepared a staement which everyone declared to be worthy of standing next to that of M. de Beaumont. He had the double advantage of appearing both for himself and for the family whose sufferings he had shared. It would have been easy for him to break his shackles at any time and walk free from the prison,

---

[191] Published by d'Alembert in 1765. The Society of Jesus was suppressed by the breve *Dominus ac Redemptor* on 21 July 1773, accusing the Jesuits of meddling in politics, of recalcitrance and of disobedience, and ordering their obliteration for ever, their houses and schools and hospitals to be closed and their novices to be dismissed and released.

[192] Monsieur de Crosne is mentioned at the beginning of this chapter as the Master of Requests. The Court of Requests (*les Requêtes de l'Hôtel*) was established in the reign of Philippe V (1294–1322) to relieve the monarch of some of his judicial duties. Masters of Requests travelled into the provinces to hear grievances voiced by the King's subjects and adjudicate on them. They also inspected local administration. The court was abolished in 1791.

simply by saying that he had left the Calas family for a brief moment at the material time when M. and Mme Calas were alleged to have been murdering their son. He had been threatened with harsh punishment; both torture and death had been presented before his eyes; one word would have restored him his freedom; but he preferred to accept torture rather than utter that word which would have been a lie. He revealed all this in detail in his statement, with such artless and simple dignity, so totally devoid of ostentation, that he moved those whom he desired only to convince, and, without seeking to impress, earned the admiration of all.

His father, a famous lawyer, had no hand in the preparation of this work; at a stroke, he found himself matched by a son who had never been called to the bar.

Meanwhile persons of the highest rank crowded into the prison, where Mme Calas had been joined by her daughters. They were moved to tears by what they saw. Humanity and nobility of heart lavished assistance upon the women; 'charity' gave them none. Charity, which is besides often mean and insulting, belonged to those of a religious disposition, and they were still very much against the Calas family.

The day finally came, on 9 March 1765, when innocence emerged triumphant. M. de Bacquencourt having been through all the proceedings and examined the case down to its smallest details, the judges unanimously pronounced the family innocent, victims of a cruel abuse of law by the Parliament of Toulouse. They rehabilitated the memory of Jean Calas. They gave leave for the family to lodge an appeal, to bring their tormentors to account, and to apply for damages with costs, which the Toulouse magistrates ought to have offered on their own initiative.

The whole of Paris erupted with joy; people gathered together in the squares, on the promenades; they flocked to see this family once heaped with misery and now so triumphantly vindicated; they applauded the judges as they passed, overwhelming them with gratitude. The spectacle was made all the more touching by the fact that this was the very day, the 9th of March, when Calas had been so cruelly put to death three years before.

The Masters of Requests had delivered complete and total justice to the Calas family, which was no more than their duty. But there is another duty, that of kindness, which is much more rarely shown in the courts, because they seem to think it is enough that they should distribute equity. The Masters of Requests determined they would write collectively to the King and beseech His Majesty to expunge, with his royal bounty, the ruin of this family. The letter was duly written. The King replied by sending thirty-six thousand livres to the mother and children; and of these thirty-six thousand, three thousand were destined for that worthy servant who had so stoutly stood by her employers and defended the truth.

By this act of kindness, as by so many others, the King earned that name bestowed upon him by the love of the nation. May his example serve to inspire tolerance among men, without which bigotry will devastate the earth, or at the very least plunge it into continuous grief and lamentation. In the present case, we are aware that we are talking of only one family, whereas thousands have perished through the madness of religious sectarianism. But now that a glimmer of peace has settled upon all Christian societies, after centuries of carnage, it is at this moment of relative tranquillity that the Calas tragedy should make a greater impression, like thunder which suddenly blasts the serenity of a fine day. Cases like this are rare, but they do happen, and they are the result of that grim superstition which persuades the weak-minded to impute a criminal character to whoever does not think as they do.

The Story of Elisabeth Canning and the Calas Family

The story of Elisabeth Canning and the Calas family

I was in London in 1753 when the case of the young Elisabeth Canning caused such a stir. Elisabeth had been missing from her parents' house for a month. She returned home an emaciated figure, dishevelled and with her clothes in tatters. 'Good heavens, what a sorry state you are in!' exclaimed her aunt. 'Where have you been? What happened to you?' 'Alas, as I was passing by Moorfields on my way home, two rough villains threw me to the ground, robbed me and took me to a house ten miles from London.'

Her aunt and neighbours wept at this story. 'My dear child, were you not brought to the house of the infamous Mrs Web, for she lives just ten miles from here?' 'Yes, my aunt.' 'A big house on the right-hand side?' 'Just so, my aunt.' The neighbours then described Mrs Web to Elisabeth, who agreed that their description fitted. One of them told her that the woman's house was a den of iniquity where young people gambled away fortunes. 'Yes, it is a truly dangerous place', replied young Elisabeth. Another commented that worse things went on there. 'Those two robbers are cousins of Mrs Web. They kidnap young girls on the public highway, give them bread and water until the girls are forced to offer their services to the gamblers who frequent the house.' 'Were you on bread and water?' asked the aunt. On hearing that she had been, they asked whether the brigands had taken advantage of her and had forced her into prostitution. She answered that she had refused, that she had been beaten for it and that her life had been in danger. At this point the aunt and the neighbours began once again to weep and wail.

Young Elisabeth was immediately taken to see Mr Adamson, who had long been the family's protector. He was a gentleman of considerable standing in the parish. Straightaway he rode off with one of his equally zealous friends to inspect Mrs Web's house. They felt certain that this was the place where the poor young girl had been kept against her will, and even concluded that a little barn used for storing hay was where she had been imprisoned. The good Adamson's feelings of compassion grew all the stronger. On his return to London he got Elisabeth to confirm that this was where she had been held. He stirred up the whole neighbourhood, and a fund was set up in aid of the victim who had been so cruelly treated.

As Miss Canning recovered her health and beauty, more and more people rallied to her side. Mr Adamson lodged a complaint with the sheriff naming her as the injured party. Mrs Web and her associates, who were living quietly in the country, were arrested and put in prison.

The sheriff, to examine the truth of the matter, summoned a young maid belonging to Mrs Web's household and asked the girl in tones of gentle kindness to tell him all she knew. This servant, who had never seen Miss Canning in all her life nor had even heard of her, ingenuously replied that she knew nothing at all about the matter. But when the sheriff told her that she would have to appear before a court of law and that she would certainly be hanged if she did not confess, she told them all they wanted to hear: so, after the jury finally met, nine persons were condemned to death.

Fortunately there are no secret trials in England, because the punishment of crime is intended as a form of public instruction and not as a private act of revenge. All questioning of witnesses takes place in open court, and the proceedings of all trials of any consequence are published in journals.

Furthermore England has preserved an old French law which prevents any criminal from being executed without the case first having been presented to the king, who must sign the death warrant. This wise, humane and necessary law, like so many others, has fallen into neglect in France, although it is observed throughout most of Europe. It is still in practice in present-day Russia, and also in China, that homeland of good morality, which laid down such sacred laws well before Europe even had civilised customs.

The time was approaching for the nine accused to be executed when the Sessions Paper fell into the hands of the philosopher Ramsay. He read the account of the trial, which he found quite farcical. It made him so indignant that he wrote an article pointing out that the first duty of a juror is to possess common sense. He remarked that Mrs Web, her two cousins and the rest of the household had to be quite extraordinary if they thought that a diet of bread and water would turn young girls into prostitutes; that, on the contrary, they would have fed and dressed them well had they wanted to make them attractive, since merchants do not soil or spoil the goods they want to sell. He argued that Miss Canning had never been in that house, and had merely repeated what her stupid aunt had suggested to her. According to Ramsay, the overzealous Adamson had instigated this ridiculous trial, which was going to cost the lives of nine innocent citizens, simply because Miss Canning was pretty and had told a lie.

The young maid, who had cooperated with the sheriff by admitting something which was not true, had not found herself able to retract her statement. Anyone who has borne false witness, either through excessive keenness or out of fear, usually stands by it or continues to lie, afraid of being known as a liar in public.

It is pointless, in Ramsay's opinion, for the law to require evidence from at least two witnesses before a person can be hanged. If the lord chancellor and the archbishop of Canterbury both testified that they had seen me assassinate my father and my mother and eat them whole for my breakfast in less than a quarter of an hour, then the chancellor and the archbishop would need to be sent to a lunatic asylum rather than that I should be put to death on account of their fine testimony. It does not matter how many witnesses and arguers you have to an absurd and impossible happening: the very impossibility of the event must outweigh all that testimony and all those arguments.

This little pamphlet opened the eyes of the sheriff and the jury. They were obliged to revise their judgment: Miss Canning was found to be a little hussy who had in fact given birth to a child at the very time when she claimed to have been held captive in Mrs Web's house. All London, which had been on her side, was as ashamed as it had been when a charlatan, boasting in front of two thousand spectators that he could put himself inside a two-pint pot, ran off with their money and left them with an empty bottle.

It may be that some details of this occurrence are incorrect, but the main facts here are known to be true by the whole of England.

This ridiculous affair would have had a truly tragic end had not a philosopher chanced to read the relevant documents in the public domain. If only there had been such a philosopher among all those white penitents in Toulouse, where an equally absurd but a thousand times more hideous trial took place! We would not now be lamenting the innocent blood that prejudice has caused to be spilt.

However, there was in Toulouse a wise man who raised his voice against the clamour of the enraged populace and against the bias of the magistrates. This man, to whom so much praise is due, was Monsieur de Lassalle, a councillor in the parlement and thus appointed to be one of the judges in the case.

He began by pointing out the irregularity of the monitory. He severely condemned the haste with which three memorial services had been held in honour of a man whose body should probably have been dragged through the streets in shame: he declared that they should not bury as a Catholic and canonise as a martyr someone who to all appearances had committed suicide and who was certainly not a Catholic. It was public knowledge that the lawyer Chalier had testified that Marc-Antoine Calas, far from being about to abjure his faith, was on the contrary intending to go to Geneva and apply to be admitted as a Protestant pastor.

Jean-Pierre Caseing, according to Lassalle, had in his possession a letter from Marc-Antoine in which the latter accused his brother Louis of desertion for having become a Catholic. Our deserter, he states in this letter, is causing us much upset. The parish priest of Saint Etienne had reported as fact that Marc-Antoine had approached him to obtain a certificate proving his Catholicism, but he, as a priest, had not wished to get involved in the corrupt practice of giving such certificates to Protestants.

Councillor de Lassalle weighed up all these points; he added in particular that, in accordance with the provisions of existing ordinances and with those of Roman law followed in Languedoc, 'there is no evidence of any kind which could allow a father to be regarded as guilty of the murder of his son and so outweigh the natural and sacred presumption which protects fathers from any such suspicion'.

Finally this worthy magistrate found that neither young Lavaisse, who had nothing to do with this frightful business, nor the Catholic servant of the family, could be accused of the alleged murder of Marc-Antoine; they should be regarded as witnesses, and their vitally important evidence should not be withheld from the accused.

Basing his opinion on such powerful arguments and moved by his sense of justice and pity, Monsieur de Lassalle spoke out with all the zeal of his humanity and his convictions. One of the judges said to him: 'Sir, you are infatuated with the Calas family.' To which Lassalle replied: 'And you, sir, are infatuated with the mob.'

It is very sad that this nobility of heart should only have served to hasten the misfortune of the family whose just cause he was defending: for, having set out his position so clearly and in public, he felt obliged to withdraw from the case, and the Calas family lost an enlightened judge who would probably have enlightened the others.

On the other hand, Monsieur Laborde, who had declared himself to be in agreement with popular prejudice, and who, on account of his extreme fervour against the Calas family, had also disqualified himself as a judge, retired to his country house near Albi, only to return from it in order to condemn Calas to the wheel.

There was, as has already been said and will continue to be said, no conclusive proof of the guilt of this family. The whole case against them rested on the flimsiest circumstantial evidence, to the everlasting shame of human reason.

The honourable Monsieur David, a capitoul or senior magistrate of Toulouse, consulted the executioner as to how Marc-Antoine Calas had come to be hanged; so it was the opinion of the executioner which led to the death sentence, while the views of the lawyers were entirely neglected.

When the time came for judgment, the reporting judge only considered the case against the father of the family, Jean Calas, and pronounced that this innocent man 'should be subjected to the Question[1], both ordinary and extra-ordinary, until he confess his accomplices, that he should then be broken alive on the wheel, where he should remain for two hours, and that finally he should be burnt at the stake'.

This opinion was supported by six judges: three others were in favour only of torture, while another two were of the opinion that an investigation should be carried out to determine whether or not Marc-Antoine could have hanged himself. A single judge determined that Jean Calas should be set free. At last, after much discussion, the majority decided in favour of torture and the wheel.

This feeble old man, aged sixty-eight, who had never quarrelled with anyone, who had never laid a hand on any of his children, was condemned to die in the most horrible fashion for having supposedly strangled and subsequently hanged with his weak and swollen hands a robust and healthy son in an act of hatred for the Catholic religion, a son who in fact had no more interest in Catholicism than his father.

Questioned about his accomplices while he was being tortured, he replied as follows: 'Where there is no crime, how can there be accomplices?'

Calas showed the same serenity and calm when he was taken from the torture chamber to the scaffold. Those who saw him pass by were touched by the spectacle: even the ordinary people, no longer gripped by religious fanaticism, shed tears over his fate. The official who presided at the execution was the last interrogator and received the same answers. Father Bourges, a Dominican and a professor of divinity, together with Father Caldaguès, a priest of the same order, were appointed to assist him in his last moments and also to persuade him to tell the truth. They found the old man resigned to the will of Providence, ready to give his life to God in repentance for his sins, but still firm in the defence of his innocence and that of the others accused with him.

He let out one cry at the first blow he received but was otherwise silent. As he waited on the wheel for the moment which would end his life, the only words he spoke were full of Christian charity: he did not attack his judges, nor did he blame them for his death. They must have been misinformed, he said. When the moment arrived for the executioner to put an end to his suffering, his last words to Father Bourges were these: 'I die an innocent man. Jesus Christ, who was innocence itself, met a far more cruel end. I have no regrets in this life and hope to leave it for eternal happiness. I feel sorrow for my wife and my son, but that

---

[1] See note 8 of the *Treatise* (above).

poor young stranger, Monsieur Lavaisse's son, whom I thought to favour by inviting him to dine, this still causes me distress.'

As he was uttering these words, the capitoul approached. The instigator of this catastrophe wished to be present at the death of Calas even though he had no official reason to be there. He cried out: 'You wretched man! Look at the faggots that will burn your body to ashes and tell the truth!' The only reply Calas gave was to turn his head away slightly, and at that moment the executioner went to work and ended his life.

In spite of the fact that Jean Calas died a Protestant, Father Bourges and Father Caldaguès were full of praise for him: 'he died in the manner of our martyrs' was what they said to those who would listen. And when it was rumoured that Calas had repented and confessed to the crime he was alleged to have committed, Father Bourges felt it his duty to tell the judges personally of the last words spoken by Jean Calas and to assure them that he had continued to protest his innocence and that of the others accused with him.

After this extraordinary execution the trial of his son, Pierre Calas, began. He was considered to be the most guilty of the remaining defendants for the following reason. A young man called Cazères had been called to Montpellier to testify to the enquiry into Marc-Antoine's death. His testimony was that, as a shop boy employed by a tailor named Bou, whose premises adjoined the Calas house, he had seen Pierre enter the shop one day. Then, according to Cazères, when Bou's daughter heard the bell ring for benediction and ordered the employees to go and attend, Pierre Calas had uttered these words: 'That's all you think about. People can find salvation in both religions. Two of my brothers think as I do. If I thought that they wanted to change religion, I would be ready to kill them. And if I had been in my father's place when my brother Louis became a Catholic, I would not have spared him.'

Why summon this witness from Montpellier to testify to something which, on the witness's own admission, took place in the presence of Mademoiselle Bou and two employees, all of whom resided in Toulouse? Why was no attempt made to hear their evidence, since the Calas family had claimed in their defence that Bou's daughter and the employees strongly affirmed that everything Cazères had impudently said was just a lie dictated to him by the enemies of the accused and the hatred of the opposition? Can one really believe that Cazères heard what was said in public to his masters when his masters and his co-workers did not hear it? And yet the judges listened to him and not to the others who were present.

Is it not evident that the testimony of the wretched fellow contains a contradiction in terms? 'One can find salvation in both religions'; that is to say that God takes pity on human error and human weakness, but I will have no pity for my own brother! God accepts the vows of anyone who addresses him sincerely, but I will kill anyone who worships him in a way which does not please me! Is it possible to conceive of a speech filled with such frightful madness?

Another far less important witness who testified that Pierre Calas had spoken ill of the Roman Catholic religion began by saying, 'I hate all Protestants!' A fine piece of admissible evidence indeed!

This was all that could be raked up against Pierre Calas. The reporting judge believed that he had discovered enough proof to send him to penal servitude for life, but he was alone in his opinion. Several judges considered that Pierre should be released, while others thought that he should be sentenced to permanent exile. The reporting judge bowed to this view, which prevailed.

The judges then came to consider Madame Calas, the virtuous widow and mother. There was no evidence at all against her, but in spite of this the reporting judge recommended exile. All the others were in favour of releasing her. Next it was the turn of young Lavaisse. What he was suspected of amounted to the height of absurdity. How could a youth of only nineteen years, living in Bordeaux, come to be chosen as the executioner of a Protestant in Toulouse? Would Madame Calas have said to him, 'You have arrived at just the right moment, we need to murder our eldest son; you are his friend, you will dine with him and afterwards you will hang him. One of our friends was to have come to dinner and would have helped us, but we will do without him'?

Such a ridiculous argument could not be sustained for much longer, but the reporting judge thought that Lavaisse deserved to be sentenced to exile. All the others, with the exception of Darbou, disagreed.

Finally, when it was the turn of the servant of the Calas family, the general opinion was that she should be set free on account of her Catholic faith. This was carried unanimously.

Is it possible that there are still judges in Toulouse who are not saddened by this harsh treatment of an innocent family? They must be shedding tears of remorse and be heartily ashamed. One sign that they are repenting their cruel decision is the fact that, for four months, they have refused to divulge details of the trial and of the judgment to all those who have asked for them.

Deep down in their hearts each one is saying to himself: 'I am horrified by all the prejudice, all that biased opinion which is an insult to nature and common sense. I acknowledge that by my decision I have sentenced to death on the wheel an old man who could not have been guilty, and that by another verdict I let off all those who must have been equally guilty if such a crime were possible. I recognise that the first decision is not consistent with the second. I admit that it was wrong just to exile the son if the father was executed on the wheel, and I confess that I have to answer for the exile of the son and the terrible death of his father as well as for the six months of imprisonment endured by a virtuous mother and an innocent young man. If we have refused to disclose the record of the trial to those who have asked us for it, it is because this has been wiped out by our tears of remorse. Let us add to those tears the reparation that is due to a decent family we have plunged into grief and indigence. I will not say they have been disgraced, because disgrace is not the lot of the innocent. Let us restore to the mother the possessions which this abominable trial has stolen from her. I would add that we should beg her for forgiveness, but which of us would dare to appear before her? Let us at least receive protests from the public as the necessary consequence of such lamentable acts of injustice. We remonstrate with the king when he asks his people for aid to help him defend the realm from its enemies, so let us not be surprised if the whole of humanity admonishes us when we put to death the most innocent of men. Surely we must recognise that these remonstrances are written with the blood of this man!'

It is likely that the judges have, on occasion, harboured such thoughts as these. It would be marvellous if they could manage to express them aloud. But how they are to be pitied if they are too ashamed even to admit to these things in their innermost being![2]

---

[2] This document comes from an eye-witness who has no connection with the Calas family but who is an enemy of fanaticism and a friend of justice. [Voltaire's note]

An address to the public concerning the parricides
imputed to the Calas and Sirven families

An address to the public concerning the parricides imputed to the Calas and Sirven families

We now have in France two accusations of parricide on account of religion in the same year, and two families sacrificed by fanaticism in the name of the law. The same prejudice which stretched Calas on the wheel in Toulouse has dragged to the gallows the entire Sirven family in a jurisdiction of the same province; and the same defender of innocence who vindicated the Calas family, Monsieur Elie de Beaumont of the Paris parlement, has also vindicated the Sirvens in a memoir signed by several advocates, a memoir which demonstrates that the sentence pronounced against the Sirvens is even more absurd than the judgment passed on the Calas family.

Let us briefly set out the facts, an account of which may serve as an instruction to foreigners who have not yet been able to read the factum of the eloquent Monsieur de Beaumont.

In 1761, at the very moment when the Protestant Calas family were in prison, accused of the assassination of their son Marc-Antoine because he was supposed to be about to become a Catholic, it happened that a daughter of Paul Sirven, an officer in feudal dues at Castres, was presented to the local bishop by a woman who managed his household. When the bishop was informed that the girl was from a Calvinist family, he had her put into a kind of convent called the 'house of the Regents', where her instruction in the Catholic faith took place by means of flogging and beating. She lost her reason, escaped from her confinement, and soon after threw herself into a well outside the village of Mazamet, far from her parents' home.

The local judge reasoned as follows: in Toulouse, Calas is going to be broken on the wheel and his wife will be burnt at the stake for having hanged their son to prevent him from attending Mass; therefore, following the example of my superiors, I should do the same to the Sirvens, who doubtless drowned their daughter for a similar reason. It is true that I have no proof that the father, mother and two sisters of this girl have assassinated her, but I have heard that there is no greater proof against the Calas family; so I run no risk. It would perhaps be too much for a country judge to order breaking on the wheel and burning, but I shall have the pleasure of hanging a whole Huguenot family, and I will be paid for my trouble out of their confiscated effects. As a precaution this stupid fanatic has the corpse examined by a doctor who is as learned in medicine as the judge is in jurisprudence. The doctor, astonished at not finding the girl's stomach full of water and ignorant of the fact that it is impossible for water to enter a body from which air cannot escape, concludes that she was knocked unconscious and then thrown into the well. A local devotee assures him that all Protestant families are in the habit of doing this. At length, after many proceedings as irregular as the reasoning behind them was absurd, the judge orders the arrest of the father, the mother and the sisters of the deceased. Hearing the news, Sirven summons his friends. They are all convinced of his innocence, but, as the Calas affair had frightened the whole region, they advise Sirven not to expose himself to the fury of fanaticism. He flees with his wife and daughters in the most inclement season. The unhappy band are compelled to cross snow-covered mountains on foot: one of the daughters, who has been married for about a year, gives birth to a child on the icy road without proper assistance. Weak as she is, she has to carry her expiring infant in her arms. When the family finally reaches safety, the first news they hear is that the parents have been sentenced to death, the two sisters, declared equally guilty, have been banished for life, their entire estate has been confiscated, and they have nothing left in this world but shame and misery.

All this may be read at greater length in Monsieur de Beaumont's work, which offers a complete proof of the innocence of the victims and evidence of the most detestable injustice.

By a stroke of providence the first attempts to clear the name of Calas after his death on the wheel in Languedoc came from the mountains of Switzerland, and the Sirvens too are to be avenged from the same wilderness. The children of Calas found a refuge there at the same time as the Sirven family sought asylum. The compassionate and truly religious persons who have had the consolation of serving these two unfortunate families, and who were the first to respect their virtue and the disasters that befell them – these men were unable to present petitions for the Sirvens because the prosecution proceeded more slowly in this case and was more protracted. Furthermore, how could a family which had wandered four hundred miles from its homeland recover the necessary documents for its vindication? What could be done by a father overwhelmed by misery, a mother dying from her grief, and two daughters just as unfortunate as their parents? They were obliged to make a formal request for a copy of the charges against them, but were prevented from doing this on account of a legal formality which, however necessary it might be, often has the effect of oppressing the poor and innocent. Their frightened relatives did not dare to write to them: all that the family could find out in their exile was that they had been condemned to death at home. The public would be horrified to know how much effort and care was needed to extract some legal proof in their favour. What kind of fatality is it which dictates that oppression should be so easy and succour so difficult?

The legal process which had been used for Calas could not be used for the Sirvens, because the Calas family had been condemned by a parlement, whereas the Sirvens had only been tried by subordinate judges whose verdict comes under the jurisdiction of that parlement. We will not repeat what has already been said by the eloquent and generous Monsieur de Beaumont; but, having considered how closely these two affairs are linked in human interest, it is our opinion that it is in the same interest to attack the fanaticism which has caused them in the first place. One might argue that they are but two very obscure families; but even if the most humble of creatures dies of a disease that has long devastated mankind, this is a warning to the whole world that the poison still flourishes. All men should be on their guard, and, if there are physicians available, they should search for remedies to put an end to the very source of this universal scourge.

It may be that for legal reasons the petition of the Sirvens cannot be heard in the King's Council: but it has reached the ears of the public, and that judge of all judges has pronounced its verdict. Therefore it is to public opinion that we address this notice, and it is in the name of the public that we are now going to speak.

Examples of fanaticism in general

Mankind has always been subject to errors: but not all of these have cost lives. We may have been ignorant of the fact that the earth revolves around the sun; we may have believed in fortune-tellers and in ghosts; we may have believed that birds foretell events to come, that serpents are enchanted, that multicoloured creatures might be created by displaying objects of different hues to the mothers; we may have been persuaded that, as the moon wanes, so the marrow of the bones diminishes; that corn must rot in order to grow, etc. But such examples of folly have not resulted in persecution, discord and murder.

Other kinds of madness, however, have disturbed the earth and given rise to a deluge of blood. We do not know, for instance, exactly how many poor wretches have been delivered to the executioner by ignorant judges, calmly and without scruple condemning them to the flames on the mere suspicion of sorcery. There is not a single court in Christendom which has not been sullied by such judicial murders over the last fifteen hundred years. And if I say that more than a hundred thousand Christians have fallen victim to this idiotic and barbarous jurisprudence, and that most of them were innocent women and girls, I am probably giving a very conservative estimate.

Libraries are crammed with books relating to the laws against witchcraft. All the decisions of the judges in these cases are based on the precedents set by the magicians of Pharaoh and the Witch of Endor, as well as by possessed individuals who are mentioned in the Bible and the apostles who were sent expressly to cast out devils. No one ever dared suggest, out of pity for the human race, that in past ages God could have allowed people to be possessed by spirits and to practise sorcery and then decided to ban these things today. Such a fine distinction would have seemed criminal: what was desperately needed were victims. Christianity has always been sullied by this absurd and barbarous practice. The Fathers of the Church believed in magic, and more than fifty councils pronounced anathemas excommunicating those whose words caused devils to enter into human bodies. These mistaken views were universally regarded as sacred. Statesmen who might have disabused the people did not think of doing so. They were too immersed in their own business and afraid of the power of prejudice. They saw that this fanaticism sprang from the very bosom of religion and dared not strike down this unnatural child for fear of injuring its mother. Instead they chose to be ruled by the people's folly rather than combat it.

Princes and kings have paid dearly for this mistake of encouraging superstition in the common people. Were the people of Paris not led to believe that Henri III used sorcery in his devotions? Was magic not used on a number of occasions in the attempt to put an end to him? In fact his life was cut short more surely by the knife of a Dominican[3] than by any hell conjured up by conspiring sorcerers. And what of the rogues who wanted to send a possessed woman like Marthe Brossier to Rome so that she could accuse Henri IV, in the name of the devil, of not being a good Catholic? Every year, in those half-savage times we are speaking of, there occurred such things. Did not the rump of the Catholic League in Paris proclaim that the devil had wrung the neck of the beautiful Gabrielle d'Estrées?

People say that one should not resurrect these stories which so dishonour human nature. But I say that we should repeat them a thousand times until they remain firmly in mankind's memory. We should for instance continue to repeat that the unfortunate priest Urbain Grandier[4] was condemned to be burnt by ignorant judges who were in the pay of a bloodthirsty minister. Grandier's

---

[3] Henri III was murdered by Jacques Clément in 1589.   [4] The curé of Loudun (1590–1634).

innocence was clear to see, but some nuns declared that he had bewitched them, and this was enough to condemn him. God was forgotten, only the devil was spoken of. Once priests had turned man's relations with the devil into an article of faith and judges deemed this imaginary crime to be as real and as frequent as theft, then it was a necessary consequence that more sorcerers would be found amongst us than thieves.

Bad law increases crime

Thus it came about that our religious rites and our jurisprudence based on the *Decretum* of Gratian[5] laid the foundations for magic. The ignorant populace reasoned as follows: our priests excommunicate and exorcise those who have made pacts with the devil; our judges burn them; it is therefore certain that bargains can be made with the devil. Now, if these bargains are made secretly, and if Beelzebub keeps his word, we will become hugely rich in a single night. All we have to do is to go to the witches' sabbath; the fear of being discovered should not outweigh our expectation of the great fortune the devil can provide. Besides, Beelzebub, being more powerful than our judges, may help us if we are caught. This is the way these wretches thought; so that the more the fanatical judges lit fires for burning, the more there were idiots to be found who were prepared to brave them.

The accusers, however, continued to outnumber the guilty. If a girl became pregnant and the name of her lover was not known, it was assumed that this was the devil's work. If some farmers obtained a more plentiful harvest than their neighbours through hard labour, they were considered to be sorcerers. The Inquisition burnt them and sold their estates for its own profit. In Germany and elsewhere in Europe judges were empowered by the pope to hand over their victims to the secular authorities, so that over a long period they acted as constables and executioners for the priesthood. This is still the case in Spain and Portugal.

The more a province was backward and ignorant, the more the devil seemed to prevail. There is a collection of decrees issued in the Franche-Comté region against sorcerers which was published in 1607, with the approval of several bishops, by the chief judge at Saint-Claude, a certain Boguet. Were someone to write such a work nowadays, he would be put into a lunatic asylum; but at that time all judges were as insane and as cruel as he was. Every province had a similar register. When at length philosophers began to bring about some enlightenment, the persecution of witches ceased, and they disappeared from the face of the earth.

[5] A twelfth-century Italian author whose work is the basis of canon law.

Concerning parricides

I venture to say that this is also true in the case of parricides. If only the judges in Languedoc would cease to believe so rashly that every father of a Protestant family sets out to murder his children as soon as he suspects that they have some leaning towards the Catholic faith, then there would be no more prosecutions for parricide. This crime is even more rare than that of making a pact with the devil; for it may happen that some feeble-minded women, given to believe by their parish priest in his sermon that it is possible to copulate with a goat at a witches' sabbath, are filled with the desire to attend a sabbath and have intercourse with a goat. They rub themselves with ointment before going to bed, and dream that they have received favours from the devil. This is only natural, but it is not natural for mothers and fathers to cut their children's throats in an effort to please God. However, if the suspicion is allowed to persist that it is common for Protestants to murder their children in order to stop them from becoming Catholics, then the Catholic religion is likely to become so odious to them as to stifle their naturally good instincts, with the result that some unfortunate fathers might actually be tempted to commit the outrageous crime of which they have so rashly been accused.

An Italian author relates that a monk in Calabria saw fit to go from village to village preaching against bestiality, which he depicted so vividly that three months later more than fifty women were accused of this hideous crime.

Tolerance alone can make society tolerable

What a dreadful passion is that pride in us which would have others think as we do! But is it not the height of folly to believe we can convert them to our way of thinking by continually subjecting them to the most malicious slanders, by persecuting them, by sending them to the galleys, by sentencing them to die from the gibbet, or on the wheel, or at the stake?

An Irish priest has recently written in a little-known pamphlet,[6] and claims this to be the opinion of others, that we come a hundred years too late to raise our voice against the lack of tolerance, that barbarity has given way to moderation, and that it is no longer the time for complaint. I say this in reply to those who speak in such terms: observe what is happening before your very eyes, and if you have any humanity you will join us in compassion and protest. Eight unfortunate preachers have been hanged in France since 1745. The bills of confession have caused much trouble and misery. Lastly a wretched fanatic from the dregs of society[7] attempted to assassinate the king in 1757, and confessed at

---

[6] The Kehl editors suggest that this might be J. T. Needham (1713–81).
[7] Damiens, who made an attempt on Louis XV's life.

his first interrogation that he had acted on his religious principles, adding these words: 'he who does good only for himself is good for nothing'. Where did he find such language? Who taught a mere college servant, a miserable valet, to use such terms? When tortured, he maintained not only that his assassination attempt was a 'meritorious deed', but that in the great hall of the Palace of Justice he had heard all the priests say the same thing.

So the contagious disease of fanaticism still thrives. The poison is so far from being eradicated that a priest from the same region as Calas and Sirven published, just a couple of years ago, a *Defence of the Massacre of Saint Bartholomew*.[8] Another has published a *Justification of the Murderers of Urbain Grandier*. When that useful and humane *Treatise on Tolerance* came out in France, copies of it were not allowed to be sold in public. This treatise has in truth done some good. But in his treatment of the barbarities of religion the author has omitted many features which would have made the picture even darker and its message all the more striking.

The author has been criticised for going a little too far when, in order to show that persecution is both detestable and senseless, he invents a descendant of Ravaillac proposing a plan to Le Tellier to poison all Jansenists.[9] This fiction would appear to be grossly exaggerated to anyone who is unacquainted with the wild excesses of fanaticism, but the reader will be surprised to learn that what is fiction in the *Treatise on Tolerance* is really historical fact.

Indeed, in the *History of the Reformation in Switzerland*, we find that priests who wanted to prevent this great change from taking place actually bribed a young servant girl to poison three of the principal supporters of reform. But since the poison used was not powerful enough, they put a stronger one into the Communion bread and wine so as to exterminate in a single morning all the adherents of the new religion and thus to ensure victory for God's Church.[10]

The author of the *Treatise on Tolerance* has also declined to mention the terrible persecution which led to the death of so many unfortunates in the valleys of Piedmont. Equally he has passed over in silence the massacre of six hundred inhabitants of Valtelina, men, women and children murdered by Catholics in September 1620. I will not go so far as to say that this happened with the consent and support of the archbishop of Milan, who was subsequently made a saint. Some ardent writers have claimed this to be the case, which I am far from believing to be true. Nevertheless I do say that there is scarcely a town or burgh in Europe where blood has not been shed as a result of religious quarrels. I say that the human species has been significantly reduced by it, because women and children were massacred as well as their menfolk: Europe

---

[8] Caveyrac, whose work appeared in 1758.
[9] See note 169 of the *Treatise*.
[10] Ruchat, I, 2–7; Roset, III, 13; Savion, III, 126; Chouet, p. 26. [Voltaire's note]

would be one-third more populous if there had been no theological disputes. Finally let me say that, instead of forgetting these abominable times, we should have them frequently put before us so that they may forever inspire a sense of horror. It is up to our century to make amends, through toleration, for this long series of crimes that intolerance has committed over sixteen hundred barbarous years.

It should not be said, therefore, that there are no traces of that shocking fanaticism associated with lack of tolerance. These traces are to be seen everywhere; they exist in those very countries which are often considered to be the most tolerant. Were Lutheran and Calvinist ministers to be in charge, they would perhaps be just as pitiless, just as hard, just as overbearing as they accuse their opponents of being. The barbarous law by which no Catholic may reside for more than three days in certain Protestant countries has yet to be revoked. An Italian, an Austrian and a Frenchman are not allowed to own a house or even an acre of land in some Protestant territories, whereas a citizen of Geneva or Schaffhausen is at least permitted to purchase a manor in France. If a Frenchman, on the other hand, wanted to buy an estate in the Protestant republics I am referring to, and if the government there wisely turned a blind eye, there would still be some evil-minded spirits who would rise up and decry this act of tolerance and humanity.

What principally foments intolerance, hatred and injustice

One of the main causes of intolerance and the hatred of citizens for their fellow countrymen is the abominable practice of perpetuating divisions between people by the use of festivals and monuments. One such custom is the annual procession in Toulouse in which God is solemnly praised for the murder of four thousand inhabitants; it has been banned several times by royal decree, and yet it has still not been abolished. Every year, in the name of piety, religion and the throne are insulted by the barbarous ceremony. This has been going on for a hundred years, which only increases the insult. Because these celebrations are such age-old ones the city of Toulouse has asked the pope for a plenary indulgence for participants in the procession. Indulgence is doubtless what it needs, but certainly does not deserve so long as it promotes fanaticism.

The last ceremony took place in 1762 at the very time that Calas was dying on the wheel. On the one hand God was being praised while, on the other, an innocent man was being slaughtered. Future generations will scarcely believe the exaggerated forms our superstition has taken in these wretched rites.

The cobblers lead the procession in ceremonial dress, carrying an effigy of the head of the first bishop of Toulouse, a prince of Peloponnesus who apparently held the see before the death of Christ! Then come the tilers with the bones of all the children put to death by Herod seventeen hundred and sixty-six years ago; though these children, as everyone knows, were buried in Ephesus, like the eleven thousand virgins in Cologne, they were nonetheless enshrined in Toulouse. The dealers in second-hand clothes display a piece of the Virgin's dress. The relics of Saint Peter and Saint Paul are carried by the tailors' guild. After this thirty corpses appear in the procession. It would not be so bad if these sights were the end of the matter: after all, piety deceived is nonetheless piety, and the foolish populace may still be a dutiful citizenry (especially when public order is well maintained), even though they carry in procession the bones of all those children murdered on the command of Herod in Bethlehem. But so many dead bodies, whose only function on this day is to reawaken memories of four thousand citizens put to death in 1562, must necessarily have a most harmful effect on the minds of the living. Add to this the black and the white penitents marching with a mask over their faces so that they resemble ghosts, and the horror of this lugubrious festival is greatly increased. People leave it with their heads full of phantoms, their hearts seized by the spirit of fanaticism, and filled with bitterness against their brethren, for whom this procession is deeply offensive. This is how in former times people would leave the so-called chambers of meditation of the Jesuits: the imagination is fired by such scenes, and hearts become hardened and cruel.

Unhappy mortals! May you have festivals which soften your manners and turn you towards clemency, gentleness and charity. Celebrate the battle of Fontenoy when all the enemy wounded were carried with our own men into the same houses, were brought into the same hospitals where they were treated with the same care and attention. Celebrate the generosity of the English who started a fund for our prisoners in the last war. Celebrate the benefactions made to the Calas family by Louis XV, and let this be an eternal reparation for an act of injustice! Celebrate the beneficent and useful institutions of the Invalides, of the ladies and gentlemen of Saint-Cyr and the Ecole militaire.[11] Let your festivals commemorate virtuous deeds but not those of hatred, discord, bloodshed and carnage!

Strange causes of intolerance

Imagine that all these things were told to a Chinaman or an Indian of good sense and that he had the patience to listen to them. Suppose that he wanted to find out why there has been so much persecution in Europe, why such inveterate

---

[11] Saint-Cyr was the convent school founded in 1686 by Madame de Maintenon for young ladies of noble birth but limited means. The Ecole militaire was founded in 1751 by Louis XV for the sons of gentlemen with small means or of those who had died in battle. The Hôtel des Invalides was a hospital for disabled soldiers built on the orders of Louis XIV in 1670.

hatred still erupts, why there has been so much animosity, why so many pastoral instructions have been issued which are little more than defamatory libel, why so many *lettres de cachet*[12] filled the prisons in the reign of Louis XIV. An answer will have to be given. Blushing with shame we will make the following reply. Some believe in enabling grace, others in efficacious grace. In Avignon they say that Jesus died for all of us, while in a suburb of Paris they say that he died for a few. In one place marriage is considered to be a visible sign of an invisible thing, in another it is claimed that there is nothing invisible in this union. There are cities in which the appearance of matter may subsist without the apparent matter existing, and where a body can be in a thousand different places at the same time. There are other cities where matter is thought to be penetrable; and to crown it all, there are in these cities great institutions where one thing is taught and other institutions where quite the opposite must be believed. The manner of argument will vary according to whether one is dressed in white or grey or black, or whether one is wearing a cloak or a chasuble. These are the reasons for this mutual lack of tolerance which causes the subjects of the same state to be constantly at odds with one another, and by an unaccountable madness these seeds of discord are allowed to persist.

The man from India or China will be quite perplexed as to how people could have been persecuted and murdered for centuries on account of this. He would immediately think that such frightful butchery could only have its source in a fundamental clash of moral principles. He will then be very surprised to learn that we all have the same moral code, the same which was professed at all times in India and China, and by which all peoples have been governed. How he must pity and despise us to see that we have been neither united nor rendered more peaceful by this universal and eternal morality. Instead scholastic subtleties have made monsters of those who, had they stuck simply to this moral code, would have been brothers.

Everything I have been saying here on the occasion of the Calas and Sirven affairs should have been said again and again during these past fifteen hundred years, from the quarrels of Athanasius and Arius (which the emperor Constantine considered to be quite insane) to those between the Jesuit Le Tellier and the Jansenist Quesnel.[13] There is not a single theological dispute which has not had disastrous consequences. Twenty volumes could be compiled from them, but I will conclude by referring to the dispute between the Franciscans and the Dominicans which paved the way for the reformation of the powerful republic of Berne. Among countless similar stories this is the most horrible, the most sacrilegious and, at the same time, the best known.

---

[12] *Lettres de cachet* were letters sealed with the king's privy seal, usually directing the imprisonment or exile without trial of the persons named.

[13] See note 170 of the *Treatise*.

A digression on the sacrileges which brought about the reformation of Berne

It is well know that the Cordeliers or Franciscans and the Jacobins or Dominicans have detested each other ever since they were founded. They were divided on several points of theology as well as being financial rivals. Their chief quarrel turned on the state of Mary before her birth. The Franciscans argued that Mary had not sinned in her mother's womb, while the Dominicans were of the opposite opinion. There never was, perhaps, a more ridiculous question, and yet it was this very matter which made these two religious orders quite irreconcilable.

A Franciscan, preaching at Frankfurt in 1503 on the immaculate conception of Mary, happened to see a Dominican called Vigan come into his church. 'I thank the Holy Virgin', he exclaimed 'for not having permitted me to belong to a sect which dishonours her and her son.' Vigan replied that this was a falsehood. The Franciscan then came down from the pulpit, carrying an iron crucifix, and struck the Dominican such a violent blow that he almost killed him, after which he went on to finish his sermon on the Virgin.

The Dominicans held a meeting to plan their revenge, and, in the hope of heaping greater humiliation on the Franciscans, they resolved to perform miracles. After several fruitless attempts they finally found a favourable opportunity in Berne.

One of their monks was confessor to a simple-minded young tailor named Jetzer, who was particularly devoted to the Virgin Mary and to Saint Barbara. This imbecile seemed to them to be an excellent subject for miracles. His confessor convinced him that the Virgin and Saint Barbara expressly commanded him to become a Dominican and to give all his money to the order. Jetzer obeyed and took the habit. When his vocation had been well tested, four Dominicans, whose names appear in the subsequent trial, disguised themselves on several occasions as best they could, one as an angel, another as a soul in purgatory, a third as the Virgin Mary and the fourth as Saint Barbara. At the end of these apparitions, which it would be too tedious to describe in detail, the Virgin finally revealed to Jetzer that she was born in original sin; that she would have been damned if her son, who was not yet on this earth, had not taken care to regenerate her immediately after she was born; that the Franciscans were impious and had grievously offended her son by claiming that his mother had been conceived without mortal sin, and that she charged him to announce this to all the servants of God and Mary in Berne.

Jetzer did not fail to do this. Mary appeared again, accompanied by two robust and vigorous angels. She thanked him and said that she had come to imprint upon him the holy stigmata of her son as proof of his mission and as a reward. The two angels tied Jetzer up and the Virgin drove nails into his hands and feet. The next day Brother Jetzer was exhibited on the altar for all to see, freshly bleeding from the heavenly favours he had received. The devout flocked to kiss his wounds. He performed as many miracles as he wanted, but the apparitions still continued. Finally Jetzer recognised the voice of the sub-prior beneath the mask he wore. He cried out and threatened to reveal everything. He followed the sub-prior into his cell, where he found his confessor and the two angels, who were entertaining some girls.

The monks, now that they were unmasked, had only one course open to them, which was to poison Jetzer. They sprinkled a communion wafer with some corrosive which had such a foul taste that Jetzer could not swallow it. He fled from the church crying out against the sacrilegious poisoners. The trial lasted for two years and came before the bishop of Lausanne because at that time laymen were not allowed to judge monks. The bishop sided with the Dominicans. He decided that the apparitions were real and that Jetzer was an imposter; he was even so cruel as to sentence the poor man to torture. But later the Dominicans imprudently degraded Jetzer, stripping him of his monk's habit. This meant that Jetzer was now a layman again and his case could therefore be heard by the Council of Berne. As a consequence of his testimony the long catalogue of crimes was confirmed. When the ecclesiastical judges were called in from Rome, they were compelled to deliver up the criminals to the secular authorities. The guilty were burnt at the Marsilly gate on 31 May 1509. Records of the trial are now in the archives of Berne and have been printed on several occasions.

The effects of bigotry and fanaticism

If a simple dispute between monks could produce such strange abominations, let us not be surprised at the multitude of crimes which bigotry has given rise to within so many rival sects. Let us continue to dread those extremes to which fanaticism leads. If we leave this monster at liberty, if we cease to cut its claws and break its teeth, if reason remains silent when it is persecuted, then we shall see the same evils perpetrated as in past ages. The seed is still there; if you let it grow it will spread over the whole earth.

So, wise readers, judge which is best: to worship God in a simple manner, to carry out all one's social duties without discussing questions that are as incomprehensible as they are dangerous, and to be just and charitable without belonging to any faction; or on the other hand to surrender to far-fetched beliefs which lead the feeble-minded towards a destructive enthusiasm and to hateful acts of atrocity.

I do not think I have digressed from my subject in relating all these examples, in recommending to men the religion which unites them rather than that which divides; the religion which is not bigoted, which forms virtuous citizens and not worthless scholars; the religion which is tolerant and does not persecute; the religion which says that the only law consists in loving God and one's neighbour rather than that which makes God into a tyrant and turns neighbours into victims. Let us not make religion resemble those nymphs of legend who copulated with animals and brought forth monsters.

Humanity has principally been perverted by monks. The wise and profound Leibniz has proved this conclusively. He has shown that the tenth century, which has been called the iron age, was in fact far less barbarous than the thirteenth and later centuries which produced that horde of parasites who vowed to live at the expense of laymen and to torment them. Enemies of the human race, enemies of one another and of themselves, these monks were incapable of knowing the delights of society and thus detested it. They lead lives of severe austerity; each one groans under this yoke, yet each one perversely makes it harder for himself. Every monk tries to shake off the chain he has forged, strikes his brother with it and is struck in his turn. Miserable as they are in their holy seclusion, they desire to make others miserable. Their cloisters are the abode of repentance, discord and hatred. Their secret domain lies in Morocco and in Algiers. They punish with imprisonment for life those brethren who may accuse them. Lastly they invented the Inquisition.

Among all those wretches who have infected half of Europe and who at the tender age of fifteen have been forced into cloisters either by poverty, ignorance or seduction, there have been, I admit, men of singular merit rising above their profession to be of service to their country. But I would go so far as to say that all the great men whose merit reached out from the cloister into the world beyond have been persecuted by their fellows. In these seminaries every true scholar, every man of genius, has to endure more discouragement and more humiliation from the envious than he would ever have encountered in the world outside. The ignoramus and the fanatic, who hold the purse strings, are held in higher esteem there than the greatest genius in Europe. The horror which reigns in these dark places seldom meets the eye of the layman. When it does, it bursts forth in a veritable explosion of crime. In May this year we saw eight of those wretched friars called Capuchins being accused of the murder of their superior in Paris. And yet, strange as it is to relate, fathers, mothers and daughters kneel before such men and confide in them, when they are the very scum of nature, stained with foul crime and boasting of their power to forgive sins of their own invention in the name of a God.

How often have they inspired those they call their penitents with all the atrociousness of their character! They have been the chief fomenters of the religious hatred which makes life so bitter. The judges who condemned the Calas and Sirven families made their confessions to monks; Calas was accompanied to the scaffold by two monks. These men, less cruel than their fellows, admitted that Calas, with his dying breath, summoned God as witness to his innocence. But when they were later asked to confirm this, they refused to do so for fear of being punished by their superiors for telling the truth.

When the final verdict was ultimately given in favour of the Calas family, an Irish Jesuit, believe it or not, dared to say in the most insipid of pamphlets that the defenders of the Calas family, and the Court of Requests which declared them innocent, were in fact the enemies of religion.

The Catholics' reply to these criticisms is that Protestants are equally worthy of condemnation. The murders of Servetus and Barneveldt are at least on a par with the assassination of Councillor Dubourg.[14] The death of Charles I in England could be said to equal that of Henri III. The dark deeds of the English Presbyterians and the fury of the cannibals of the Cévennes are equivalent to the horror of the massacre of Saint Bartholomew.

Look at a variety of sects across the centuries, and everywhere you will find, over sixteen hundred years, a more or less equal proportion of horror and absurdity. Everywhere the blindly intolerant destroy one another in the darkness they inhabit. What religious question is ever debated without bitterness and malice? What theological dogma has not resulted in bloodshed? This was the necessary consequence of those terrible words 'Whosoever listens not to the Church shall be regarded as a Pagan and a Publican.'[15] Each party claimed to be the true Church. Therefore each party has always reasoned in the following manner: as we abhor customs officers, so we are minded to treat whoever does not agree with us in the same way that smugglers treat those officers when they have the upper hand. It was thus that the first dogma to be established everywhere was one of hatred.

When the king of Prussia entered Silesia in 1740, a small Protestant borough, jealous of a neighbouring Catholic village, came humbly to beg permission to put all the inhabitants of that village to the sword. The king replied: 'If that village came to ask me for leave to cut your throats, would you think me right to grant it to them?' To which they replied: 'O gracious sovereign, the case is very different: we are the true Church.'

Remedies against the madness of souls

The wild fury of prejudice which leads us to consider as guilty those who do not agree with us, the madness of superstition, of persecution and inquisition – this is an epidemic that, like the plague, has prevailed at various times in history. The

[14] Servetus was condemned by Calvin, Barneveldt by the Dutch reformers. Voltaire often cites Dubourg's death as an example of Catholic fanaticism.
[15] Matthew, 18:17.

following preventive measures are known to be the most effective against this disease. Firstly, acquaint yourself with Roman law up to the time of Theodosus. You will not find a single edict which permits the torturing, the crucifying or the breaking on the wheel of anyone accused merely of not sharing your opinion, and who does not trouble society by acts of civil disobedience or by insults against the official religion as authorised by the laws of the state. This first reflection will help to alleviate the symptoms.

Then collect several passages from Cicero, beginning with this one:[16] *Superstitio instat et urget, et quocumque te verteris, persequitur*, etc. If you let superstition gain access to you, it will follow you everywhere and you will never be free from it. These words of caution will be very useful in treating the ailment we have to deal with.

Do not forget Seneca, who, in his Epistle 95, says the following: *Vis Deos propitiare? bonus esto: satis illos coluit quisquis imitatus est.* If you want God to be favourable to you, be just; we do him sufficient honour when we imitate him.

When you have got a good supply of these countless ancient remedies, pass on to the good bishop Synesius who said to those who wanted to ordain him: 'I warn you that I will neither deceive nor force the conscience of anyone, I will allow everyone to enjoy his own opinion in peace, and I shall abide by mine. I will teach nothing but what I believe. If you will ordain me on these conditions, I consent; if not, I give up the bishopric.'

Then come down to the moderns and take some medicine from Archbishop Tillotson,[17] the wisest and most eloquent preacher in Europe, who says that 'all sects are commonly most hot and furious for those things for which there is the least reason'. In another place he says this: 'Better it were that there were no reveal'd religion; and that human nature were left to the conduct of its own principles mild and merciful and conducive to the happiness of society than to be acted by a religion which inspires men with so wild a fury.'[18] Observe well these remarkable words. They do not say that human reason is preferable to revelation, but they do indicate that, in the absence of a happy medium between reason and that abuse of revelation which creates fanatics, it would be a hundred times better to yield to nature rather than to a persecuting and tyrannical religion.

I next recommend to you these verses which I have read in a work[19] that is both very pious and very philosophical:

---

[16] *De Divinatione*, II, 72. [Voltaire's note]

[17] John Tillotson (1630–94). A French translation of his *Sermons* was published in Amsterdam by Barbeyrac from 1713 to 1729. Voltaire is quoting here from the 6th Sermon.

[18] Quoted by Voltaire, in the French text, in English.

[19] This unnamed work turns out to be Voltaire's own *Poem on Natural Law*, which was published in 1756 and probably composed in Berlin in 1752.

In our religion show discreet fidelity;
Be kind, tender and wise, forbearing too like she,
And seek to lead a life that does no others harm;
Mercy is always right, it's wrong to lose our calm.
For our brief stay on earth of pain and misery,
Children of the same God, let's live fraternally;
May we aid each other to bear our heavy load.
All weigh'd down by our ills we walk along the road;
A thousand cruel foes assail us constantly,
Our lives we always curse yet cherish equally;
Our hearts have gone astray, guideless, lacking support,
Consumed by desire or with boredom distraught.
Not one of us has lived without knowing alarms.
From our society the many helpful charms
Console us in our pain, at least for an instant,
A feeble remedy for ills that are constant.
O! Let us not poison the sweetness that remains.
Methinks we are but slaves in dungeons and in chains,
Able to help ourselves, yet e'er at daggers drawn,
Fighting with the irons from which we can't be shorn.

When you have fortified your mind with a hundred such passages, go still further: become accustomed to think for yourself. Observe what you will receive by desiring to rule over other people's minds. You will be followed by a few foolish souls, but you will be abhorred by all reasonable minds. If you have a belief, you will be a tyrant to impose it on others. If you do not believe, then you are a monster to teach what you despise and to persecute those whose opinion you share. In a word, tolerance is the only remedy against the errors which pervert the minds of men from one end of the globe to the other.

The human race resembles a crowd of passengers on board a ship. Some are at the stern, others at the prow, many in the hold and in the bilges. The ship leaks on every side, the storm does not abate: the wretched passengers will all be swallowed up! Instead of giving each other the necessary assistance which would make the passage less arduous, should we make the voyage still more dreadful? Here is a Nestorian, there a Jew; one believes in an inhabitant of Picardy, another in a native of Eisleben.[20] Over here is a family of fire-worshippers, over there are Moslems, and not far away are some Anabaptists. But what does it matter to which sect they belong? They should work together to stop the ship from leaking, so that each one, by securing his neighbour's life, also secures his own. Yet they quarrel with one another and perish.

[20] Voltaire is referring here to Calvin and Luther.

134

Conclusion

After showing our readers the succession of superstitions down the centuries we call on all noble and compassionate souls who can serve as an example to others. We implore them to place themselves at the head of those who have undertaken to justify and succour the Sirven family. The shocking case of the Calas family, which has concerned the whole of Europe, cannot have exhausted the generosity of sensitive hearts; and since the most horrid injustice has spread to another case, virtuous pity will increase accordingly.

We have to say, to the glory of our age, which is one of philosophy, that the Calas family received help to repair their misfortunes only from the hands of the enlightened and the sagacious, who dare to crush fanaticism. Not one of those who are called devout, I say it with sorrow, has wiped away their tears or filled their purse. None but rational minds think nobly; crowned heads, souls worthy of their rank, have on this occasion led by example; their names will be inscribed in the records of philosophy, a philosophy which consists in the horror of superstition and in that universal charity recommended by Cicero, *caritas humani generis*. This is a charity whose name the theologians have appropriated when in reality they do their utmost to proscribe it. This charity consists in a love of mankind, a virtue unknown to impostors, to pedants who dispute and to fanatics who persecute.

An Account of the Death of the Chevalier de La Barre

An account of the death of the chevalier de La Barre

related by Mr Cassen, advocate at the King's Council,
and addressed to the Marquis de Beccaria

It would seem, Sir, that every time a benevolent spirit undertakes to render service to mankind, a wicked demon rises up immediately to undo the work of reason.

No sooner had you enlightened Europe with your excellent book on crime and punishment than someone who calls himself a legal expert wrote an attack upon it in France.[21] Where you had upheld the cause of humanity, he was the advocate of barbarity. It was perhaps this publication which played a part in the disaster befalling the young chevalier de La Barre and the even younger son of President d'Etallonde.

Before I recount this horrifying tale, which has appalled the whole of Europe (except for a few fanatical enemies of humanity), allow me first to lay down two principles which you will surely find incontrovertible.

1. Suppose a nation is still barbarous enough to submit to torture persons accused of a crime, thereby making them suffer a thousand deaths instead of one and without knowing whether they are innocent or guilty. It should at least be clear that such an extreme measure must not be used against someone who has confessed to the crime he is accused of and where there is no further need of proof.
2. It is absurd and cruel to punish with the same penalty reserved for parricides and poisoners those violations of what is merely accepted behaviour in a

---

[21] Possibly Muyart de Vouglans, who published a refutation of Beccaria's work in 1766 in spite of signing a petition in favour of La Barre in that year.

139

given society and those crimes which are simply an offence against current opinion, causing no bodily harm whatsoever.

If these two principles are not well founded, then there is neither justice nor reason on earth; mankind is left to the caprice of tyranny, and its fate is worse than that of beasts.

With these two rules firmly established I now come to the terrible story I promised you.

There lived in Abbeville, a small town in Picardy, an abbess who was the daughter of an esteemed member of the King's Council. A pleasant woman with a gentle, cheerful spirit and a kindly soul, her conduct was beyond reproach and her manner pious without a hint of fanaticism. An inhabitant of the same town, a certain Belleval, sixty years of age, was on close terms with the abbess, since he was in charge of some of her convent's business. He was the lieutenant of a small tribunal called an election (if tribunal is the proper term for a group of citizens solely appointed to administer the collection of a tax known as the *taille*). This man fell in love with the abbess. At first she rejected his advances with all her usual gentleness, but when he became too insistent she was obliged to show her aversion and disdain.

At about that time, in 1764, she invited her nephew to stay with her. The chevalier de La Barre was the grandson of a lieutenant-general in the army, but his father had squandered a fortune of more than forty thousand livres per annum. The abbess took care of this young man like a son and was prepared to obtain for him the command of a cavalry regiment. His lodgings were outside the convent, but his aunt often invited him and some of his friends to dine with her. Belleval, excluded from these invitations, took his revenge on the abbess by seeking to cause her financial embarrassment.

Young La Barre actively took his aunt's side and spoke to Belleval in a haughty manner. This so incensed Belleval that it increased his desire for revenge. He knew that La Barre and young d'Etallonde, the son of a local administrator, had recently failed to take off their hats to a religious procession: this was in July 1765. From that moment Belleval sought to spread the rumour that their momentary disregard for the proprieties was really a premeditated act of blasphemy. While he secretly hatched his plot, by an unfortunate coincidence it was discovered that, on 9 August, the wooden crucifix on the new bridge at Abbeville had been vandalised. Drunken soldiers were suspected of being the culprits of this impious deed.

I cannot refrain from remarking that it is perhaps improper and dangerous to set up on a bridge something that should be revered in a Catholic church: public vehicles can easily break it or inadvertently knock it down. Drunken revellers may insult it on their way home without even realising the impiety of their behaviour. Furthermore it should be pointed out that these vulgar objects – crucifixes on the public highway, statues of the Virgin Mary and of Jesus to be seen on street corners in several of our towns – these are not worthy of the same adoration as they are in our churches, all the more so since it is permitted to pass them by without bowing one's head. They are monuments to an unenlightened religion. In the opinion of sensible human beings, what is holy should remain in a holy place.

Unfortunately the bishop of Amiens, who was also bishop of Abbeville, gave this event an importance and a notoriety it did not warrant. He had monitories published. There was a solemn procession to the damaged crucifix, and for a whole year Abbeville was gripped by stories of sacrilegious acts. It was rumoured that a new sect had been founded which destroyed crucifixes and threw all the Eucharistic hosts on the ground and pierced them with knives. Much blood was said to have flowed from the hosts: there were women who claimed to have witnessed this. All the old slanderous stories circulated again, just as they had been uttered against the Jews throughout Europe. You know how wildly fanatical and credulous the common people become when, as always, they are led on by priests.

Belleval, seeing that people were getting very heated over this, maliciously linked the story of the crucifix to that of the religious procession, although the two were quite unconnected. He made enquiries into the whole of La Barre's past. Summoning valets, maids and common labourers, he told them, as though inspired by faith, that they were obliged by the monitories to reveal anything that could be used against this young man. They all replied that they had never heard that La Barre had had any part in the damage done to the crucifix.

No evidence came to light regarding the mutilation of the cross, and it even seemed highly doubtful whether the crucifix had been deliberately mutilated. People began to think – which was plausible enough – that some cart laden with wood had caused this accident.

To those he wanted as his witnesses Belleval said this: 'But if you are not sure that the chevalier de La Barre mutilated the crucifix as he crossed the bridge, you do know that this July he and two of his friends passed close to a religious procession without taking off their hats. You have heard it said that he once sung blasphemous songs. Therefore you will be committing a mortal sin if you do not accuse him.'

After intimidating them in this way he went to see the principal judge at the seneschal's court in Abbeville. There he testified against his enemy and forced the judge to listen to the accusers.

Once proceedings had begun, there was a flood of informers. Everyone said what they had seen or what they thought they had seen, what they had heard or imagined they had heard. But consider Belleval's surprise when the witnesses he had incited against La Barre denounced his own son as one of the main accomplices in the acts of impiety that were being brought to light! He was thunderstruck and made sure that his son escaped forthwith. However, and this you will find hard to believe, he pursued this horrible trial with no less vigour.

These, sir, were the charges brought against the accused:

On 13 August 1765, six witnesses testified that they saw three young men pass within thirty paces of a religious procession, that La Barre and d'Etallonde did not take off their hats, and that Moisnel held his hat under his arm.

In an additional piece of information, Elisabeth Lacrivel testified that she had heard from one of her cousins that this cousin had heard the chevalier de La Barre say that he had not taken off his hat.

On 26 September a commoner called Ursule Gondalier testified that she had heard it said that La Barre, when he saw a plaster figure of Saint Nicholas at the house of the convent's portress, Sister Marie, had asked her if she had bought the figure to have a man in her home.

A man called Bauvalet testified that the chevalier de La Barre had uttered an impious word when speaking of the Virgin Mary.

Claude, known as Sélincourt, gave uncorroborated evidence that the accused told him God's commandments were the work of priests; but, confronted with this, the accused maintained that Sélincourt was a liar and that they were only speaking about the commandments of the Church.

A man called Héquet, also an uncorroborated witness, testified that the accused told him he could not understand how one could worship an image of God. The accused, when questioned about this, said he had been speaking about the Egyptians.

Nicholas Lavallée testified that he had heard the chevalier de La Barre sing two blasphemous guardroom songs. The accused admitted that one day when he was drunk he had sung them with d'Etallonde, without knowing what he was saying: in truth Mary Magdalen is referred to as a whore in one song, but she had led a loose life before her conversion. He agreed that he had recited Piron's *Ode to Priapus*.

The said Héquet also testified that he had seen the chevalier genuflect in front of books entitled *Thérèse philosophe*, the *Tourière des carmelites* and the *Portier des chartreux*.[22] He did not mention any other book, but, when questioned about this and asked to verify it, he said he was not sure if it was La Barre who had genuflected.

A man called Lacour testified that he had heard the accused use an obscene

[22] All of these are well-known eighteenth-century pornographic works.

expression instead of 'in the name of the Father, etc.' La Barre denied this when questioned by the judges.

A certain Pétignot testified that he had heard the accused recite the litanies using obscene language such as one finds in Rabelais and which I dare not reproduce here. The accused denied this when he was interrogated. He admitted he had used foul words, but not to the extent reported.

That is the sum of the allegations made against La Barre, Moisnel, d'Etallonde, Douville de Maillefeu and the son of Belleval, the instigator of the whole tragic affair.

It is evident that they were not involved in any public nuisance, since La Barre and Moisnel were arrested only as a result of the monitories issued after the mutilation of the crucifix, an act of public disorder which none of the witnesses accused them of. All their past conduct was investigated, and private conversations at least a year old were referred to. Facts were collected that were quite unrelated, so that in this respect the proceedings against them were wholly contemptible.

Without these monitories and the violent behaviour of Belleval there would have been no case of an affront to public morals and no trial for these unfortunate young men. Indeed the only scandalous thing lay in the trial itself. The Abbeville monitory had exactly the same effect as the one in Toulouse against the Calas family: it led astray the hearts and minds of people. The witnesses, stirred up by Belleval as those in Toulouse had been by the capitoul David, recalled events and snippets of conversation when it was scarcely possible for anyone to have remembered clearly whether the circumstances were incriminating or not.

One has to concede, sir, that, although a monitory is sometimes necessary, at other times it is downright dangerous. It invites people of the lowest orders to accuse their social superiors, of whom they are always jealous. The Church is thus ordering people to become vile informers. You are threatened with hell if you do not put your neighbour in danger of his life.

Even in the courts of the Inquisition there is nothing perhaps so irregular as this. Serious proof of the illegality of these monitories is to be found in the fact that they do not emanate directly from the magistrates but are simply decreed by the ecclesiastical authorities. It is truly strange that an ecclesiastic who cannot pronounce a death sentence should hand to the judges the very instrument of execution which he is forbidden to wield!

The only two to be questioned were the chevalier de La Barre and Moisnel, a child of barely fifteen years. Moisnel, quite terrified, was so distraught on hearing the judge speak of an offence against religion that he went down on his knees and confessed his sins as if he were talking to a priest. La Barre, more experienced and more sure of himself, answered all the questions put to him in a cool and rational manner, and exempted Moisnel from all blame, saying that he felt pity for him. This conduct, which he maintained to the very end, proves how noble-minded he was. In the eyes of intelligent judges this should have counted for a great deal, but here it counted for nothing.

In this trial, sir, which has had such terrible consequences, you will find only improprieties and not a single evil deed. You will find not one of those offences which are deemed to be crimes in every nation of the world – no murder, no robbery with violence, no act of treachery: nothing these young men were accused of would even be considered a crime in other Christian communities. Let us assume that La Barre and d'Etallonde did say that one should not worship an image of God, but this is precisely what is said by all members of the Reformed Church.

The lord chancellor of England would pronounce those very words before the whole of Parliament without a single unfavourable reaction. When Lord Lockhart was ambassador in Paris, a regular visitor to his house smuggled in the Eucharist for one of the servants who was ill and who was a Catholic; when Lord Lockhart discovered this, he expelled the visitor and told Cardinal Mazarin that he would not tolerate such an insult. He specifically referred to the Eucharist in terms of idolatry and the worship of images. Mazarin apologised.

The great Archbishop Tillotson, the finest preacher in Europe[23] and almost the only one not to have dishonoured the art of rhetoric by the use of feeble clichés and empty bombast (like Cheminais) or by specious reasoning (like Bourdaloue) – he refers to our Eucharist in exactly the same terms as the chevalier de La Barre. So what is respectfully accepted in the mouth of Lord Lockhart in Paris and Lord Tillotson in London can only be considered, in the present case in France, as a minor infringement, an offence against current practice, a disregard for common opinion, an indiscreet piece of conversation which happened to have two or three witnesses. Is it not the height of cruelty to punish such indiscretions with the same severity meted out to someone who poisoned his parents or set fire to his native town?

Observe, sir, to what extent there are double standards here. You will find the following in the twenty-fourth Persian letter by Monsieur de Montesquieu, the esteemed president of the Bordeaux parlement and a member of the French Academy: 'This magician is called the pope: he would have us believe that three makes one, that bread is not bread, wine not wine, and many other similar things!'

Monsieur de Fontenelle wrote in similar fashion in his account of Rome and Geneva, calling these cities Méro and Enegu. There is a thousand times more scandal in the words of Fontenelle and Montesquieu – exposed as they are to the view of thousands of readers – than in the few words uttered by La Barre in the

<hr>

[23] See note 17 above.

presence of a single witness, words which have disappeared without a trace. Private conversations should be regarded in the same way as thoughts: this is a principle which even the most barbarous nation should recognise.

I will go further, sir, and say that there is no law in France according to which a person may be sentenced to death for blasphemy. The law of 1666 prescribes a fine for the first offence, which is subsequently doubled until, on the sixth occasion, the offender is put in the pillory.

Yet the Abbeville judges were so extraordinarily ignorant and cruel as to sentence the young d'Etallonde to the following punishment:

1. To suffer the ordeal of having his tongue cut off at the root. If the victim does not present his tongue for amputation, then it is forcibly pulled out with iron tongs.
2. To have his right hand amputated outside the most important church of the town.
3. To be taken to the marketplace on a cart, to be chained to a stake and to be ceremoniously burnt alive. Fortunately d'Etallonde spared his judges the horror of this execution by fleeing the country.

Because La Barre was securely in their hands, the judges had enough humanity to reduce his sentence, ordering that he should be beheaded before being thrown on to the fire. But if they lightened his ordeal in one respect, they increased it in another by condemning him to suffer torture so that he should reveal his accomplices, as though a young man's wild behaviour and a few ill-chosen words constituted a crime against the State, a major conspiracy. This astonishing sentence was pronounced on 28 February 1766.

Jurisprudence in France is in such a muddle, and consequently the ignorance of judges so great, that the decision of those who pronounced this sentence was based on a declaration of Louis XIV made in 1682, when two women called Voisin and Vigoureux, together with two priests called Vigoureux and Le Sage, committed imaginary acts of sorcery and real acts of poisoning their victims. This royal decree of 1682 does in fact prescribe the death penalty for acts of sacrilege when combined with superstition. But this law is concerned only with magic and sorcery, that is to say with those who take advantage of the people's credulity, call themselves magicians and are both profaners and poisoners. This is the spirit and the letter of that law, which, being aimed at crimes against society, has nothing to do with frivolous speech, imprudent conduct, trifles and stupidities committed without premeditation, without criminal intent and without causing any public harm.

Thus the judges at Abbeville were obviously violating the law as well as the rules of humanity by sentencing to such horrific and extraordinary punishment a nobleman and a son of a very respectable family, each at an age when their foolishness could be considered as an aberration that a year in prison would have cured. There was so little concrete evidence that the judges, in their summing-up, resorted to the vague and ridiculous expressions used by the lower orders: 'for having sung abominable and execrable songs against the Virgin Mary and against the saints'. Please note, sir, that they had sung these 'abominable and execrable' songs in the hearing of only a single witness, whose testimony they had every right to challenge. Are these epithets really worthy of the magistrature? An old drinking-song is, after all, just a song. What is truly abominable and execrable is the mindless spilling of blood, the torturing, the pulling out of a tongue, the cutting off of a hand, the burning at the stake.

The seneschal's court at Abbeville comes under the jurisdiction of the Paris parlement. The chevalier de La Barre was therefore transferred to Paris and his case examined there. Ten of the most distinguished Parisian lawyers signed a report which demonstrated the illegality of the proceedings and pointed out that leniency should be shown to minors who are not accused either of premeditated crime or of conspiracy. The procurator-general, a man well versed in law, was minded to quash the Abbeville verdict. There were twenty-five judges, ten of whom agreed with this opinion. The other fifteen, owing to circumstances I cannot put in writing, felt obliged to uphold this astonishing verdict, which they did on 4 June 1766.

It hardly seems possible, sir, that in a civilised society a majority of five out of twenty-five should be enough to take away the life of an accused who is very likely to be innocent. In such cases the judgment ought to be unanimous, or, at the very least, there should be a majority of three to one for the death penalty. Furthermore, if the latter is the case, then the quarter who judged in favour of a more lenient sentence should be allowed to prevail over the other three-quarters, made up of cruel citizens who trifle with the lives of their fellow human beings without the slightest benefit to society.

The whole of France was horrified by this judgment. La Barre was sent back to Abbeville for execution. The guards who accompanied him were told to take a circuitous route for fear that he might be rescued by his friends, something that should have been hoped for rather than feared.

So, on 1 July, this all-too-memorable execution took place in Abbeville. The young man had first to undergo the ordeal of torture. I will describe the kind of torment he suffered. The victim's legs are squeezed between wooden planks; iron wedges are then inserted between the knees and the planks until the bones are broken. The chevalier de La Barre fainted at that point, but soon regained consciousness with the aid of some spirituous liquor. He continued, uncomplainingly, to declare that he did not have any accomplices.

To hear his confession, and to assist him in his final moments, he was given a Dominican priest who was a friend of his aunt and with whom he had often dined at the abbess's convent. This good man broke down in tears and it was the chevalier who consoled him. Dinner was served, but the priest could barely touch the food. 'Let us eat a little', said the chevalier, 'for you will need strength to endure the sight of my suffering.'

The spectacle was indeed a terrible one. Five executioners had been sent from Paris to carry out the sentence of death. I cannot actually say if his tongue and hand were cut off. All I know from the letters I have received is that he mounted the scaffold with quiet courage, calm, uncomplaining and altogether dignified. All he said to the priest who attended was this: 'I never thought that a gentleman could be put to death for so little.'

He certainly would have become an excellent officer. He was studying the arts of warfare and had already made some observations on the writings of the king of Prussia and the maréchal de Saxe, the two greatest generals in Europe.

When news of his death reached Paris, the papal legate said publicly that in Rome La Barre would not have been treated in this way, and that if he had confessed his sins to the Spanish or Portuguese Inquisition he would merely have been condemned to do penance for a few years.

I leave it to you, sir, in your wisdom and your humanity, to reflect upon so frightful and extraordinary an event. All we know of the sufferings of the early Christians appears insignificant by comparison. Tell me who is the more guilty, a child who sings a couple of songs that are thought to be blasphemous by his own sect but which are considered innocent by everyone else, or a judge who incites his colleagues to put this same child to death in such a horrible manner for a mere indiscretion.

The wise and eloquent marquis de Vauvenargues has written: 'What does not injure society is not a matter for the law.'[24] This truth should be the foundation of all criminal codes. The chevalier de La Barre has certainly not harmed society by saying something imprudent to a valet and a nun at a convent gate or by singing a song. His misdemeanours amounted to no more than a few minor lapses that people barely remembered, a few long-forgotten childish pranks which were only drawn from obscurity by the monitory which brought them to light, a monitory fulminated for an entirely different purpose, creating informers by its tyranny and disturbing the peace of the families it affected.

An imprudent young man should not be treated as a hardened criminal, and the truth of this is to be seen in the fact that young d'Etallonde, sentenced by the same judges to an even more horrible death, was welcomed by the king of Prussia and given a post in his army. He is regarded by his regiment as an

---

[24] *Réflexions et maximes*, no. 164.

excellent officer. Who knows if he will not come one day to avenge the injustice he suffered in his own country?

The execution of the chevalier de La Barre threw the whole of Abbeville into such consternation and so horrified people that no one dared proceed with the trial of the remainder of the accused.

You are no doubt astonished, sir, that so many tragic incidents take place in a country which prides itself on its gentle way of life, and where strangers flock to taste the pleasures of society. But I will not conceal from you the fact that, in spite of the presence of a fair number of enlightened minds, there are many others who retain a barbarousness which nothing has been able to eradicate. You can still find the same attitude of mind which caused a price to be set on the head of a cardinal who was prime minister, and which led to the archbishop of Paris being escorted to the sanctuary of a prison at dagger point.[25] Religion was certainly more affronted by these two deeds than by the misconduct of La Barre. That, however, is the way the world works: *Ille crucem sceleris pretium tulit, hic diadema* (One received a cross for his crime, the other a crown).[26]

Some judges have said that in present circumstances religion needed an example of this kind to serve as a warning. Nothing could be more mistaken, nothing does religion more harm. This is not how people are kept in check: they are angered and revolted by it.

I have had the misfortune to hear several people say that they could not help but detest a sect which only maintains its point of view with the aid of executioners. Such frequently uttered public statements have given me cause for concern on several occasions.

This sect has wished to put to death, by a method designed for parricides and poisoners, two children accused of singing blasphemous songs. That in itself caused a thousand times more blasphemy. You cannot imagine, sir, how hateful our Roman Catholic religion appears in the eyes of all foreigners as a consequence of this event. The judges say they had to act in this manner for political reasons. What foolish and barbarous politics! What a horrible crime against justice to pass a sentence for political reasons, especially when it is the death sentence! And then again, what a death!

The shock and the horror of it prevent me from saying anything more.

[25] An allusion to Mazarin and to Retz. Cardinal Mazarin succeeded Richelieu as prime minister and retained office under Louis XIV. Retz, who became archbishop of Paris in succession to his uncle, was active in the first Fronde of 1648–9, a rebellion against the unpopular measures taken by Mazarin.

[26] Juvenal, *Satire* XIII, verse 105. [Voltaire's note]

The Cry of Innocent Blood

The cry of innocent blood

To the Most Christian King,
In his Council of State

Sire,

The august ceremony of your coronation has not augmented Your Majesty's authority: nor could the oaths you have sworn to be wise and humane increase your natural generosity of heart and your love of justice. But it is on such solemn occasions as this that the unfortunate are permitted to throw themselves at your feet. They flock to your court; this is the moment for you to show them mercy. Clemency, seated beside you on your throne, offers up all those who have suffered the wrongs of persecution. I stretch forth my arms in supplication from afar, from the depths of a foreign land. Oppressed from the tender age of fifteen (and the whole of Europe knows how horribly), I have no advocate, no support, no patron – but you are just.

My name is d'Etallonde de Morival. Of noble birth, I hail from your loyal province of Picardy. Several of my forebears died fighting for their country. I have a brother who is a captain in the Champagne regiment. From early childhood it was my wish to embark on a career in the army.

In 1765, when I was in Gelderland learning the German language and some mathematics (two skills an officer needs), I heard that I was cited on a criminal charge at the district court of Abbeville.

I was sent such unexpectedly horrifying and extraordinary details of the case against me that I resolved, in spite of my extreme youth, never to return to a town given over to intrigues and acts of trickery offensive to my character. I felt I had been born with enough courage and valour to bear arms in whatever capacity I could. With my good knowledge of German, and impressed by the military prowess of the Prussian army and the greatness of the king who had created it, I enlisted in one of his regiments.

My honesty would not allow me to hide the fact that I was a Catholic, and that I would never change my religion. This revelation did me no harm, and I can produce letters from my commanding officers which certify that I have always carried out my duties as a soldier and my obligations as a Catholic. I found the Prussians to be men of war, but never men of intolerance.

The king of Prussia, who takes an interest in all his regiments, learned that there was a young Frenchman in one of them who was reputed to be well mannered and sober-minded, who had always satisfied his superiors, and whose sole occupation, after his training exercises, was to study the art of warfare. Having seen by chance some of my plans for fortifications and encampments, for marches and battles, he honoured me with the title of aide-de-camp and military engineer. I am eternally grateful to him, and my duty is to live and die in his service. Your Majesty is too generous not to approve of such sentiments.

May it therefore please Your Majesty and his Council in their wisdom to consider now the barbarity and injustice about which I lodge my complaint.

The abbess of the convent of Willancourt in Abbeville, the much-respected daughter of a chancellor who was almost as highly esteemed as the present incumbent of that office in France, had an implacable enemy in one of the judges at the local court, a certain Duval de Soicourt. The open hostility between them, of a kind much more common in small towns than in large ones, was well known in Abbeville. On the advice of relatives, the abbess had been obliged to deprive Soicourt of the guardianship of a wealthy young girl who had been in the care of her convent.

Soicourt, who had just lost two lawsuits against families in Abbeville, swore to get his revenge. It is common knowledge to what hideous extremes he went in pursuit of this goal. The whole of Europe was horrified, and this feeling of horror, far from diminishing with the passage of time, has continued to increase.

It is generally acknowledged that Duval de Soicourt acted in Abbeville in exactly the same way as the capitoul David had behaved in Toulouse towards the innocent Calas family.[27] Your Majesty has doubtless heard of the judicial murder of the Calas family which your council has so rightly and so strongly condemned. I am beseeching you to bring your justice to bear on an act of similar barbarity.

---

[27] I must point out here (and this is important) that, in the horrifying trial initiated solely by Duval de Soicourt, Monsieur Cassen, advocate at the King's Council, was consulted. He wrote about it to the marquis de Beccaria, that foremost expert in legal matters. I have seen his published letter, in which there has been a mistake over the names involved. Belleval was written instead of Duval. There are also mistakes in some less important details of the trial. [Voltaire's note]

The generous Madame de Brou, the abbess of Willancourt, was looking after a cousin of hers, a young man who was the grandson of a lieutenant-general in your army and about my age. He too was studying military tactics, but his talents were far superior to mine. I still possess his handwritten notes on the campaigns of the king of Prussia and the maréchal de Saxe, which prove that he would have been fit to serve under either of these great men.

We became friends, sharing the same interests, and I was honoured to be invited with him to dine with the abbess in June 1765. We set off for our appointment rather late, so that we were in a great hurry. It began to rain and we happened to meet some other young men of our acquaintance. We all put on our hats and continued on our way. There was, I remember, a procession of Franciscan friars at some distance from us.

Soicourt, on hearing that we had not made a detour to kneel before the procession, had the idea of taking Madame de Brou's cousin to court on account of this. It was just to intimidate him, he said, and to show the abbess that he was a man to be reckoned with.

But when he found out that a wooden crucifix had recently been broken on the bridge at Abbeville, either by accident or because it was very dilapidated, he decided to accuse us of mutilating it, and to join this to his accusation about the procession, which was not an easy thing to do.

I have by no means exaggerated when I said that Soicourt was following in the steps of the capitoul David, for he wrote letter upon letter to the bishop of Amiens. These letters must still be amongst the bishop's papers. He maintained that there was a conspiracy against the Catholic religion, that every day crucifixes were being vandalised, that consecrated hosts had been stolen so that they could be pierced with knives, and, so it was rumoured, blood had flowed from them.

This calumny is too absurd to be believed. I do not believe it myself, even though I read it in the copies of the documents which I now have in my possession.

On the basis of these odious and extravagant statements monitories were obtained, that is to say orders to all servant girls, indeed to the whole populace, to go and disclose to the judges any fantastic story they might have heard about the conduct of others, and to make slanderous accusations under oath, or else they would be damned.

An important fact about the case, which I myself had not been aware of, was certainly unknown to those considering it in Paris. Duval de Soicourt, who had intimidated the whole of Abbeville, alarmed all its families, and forced the abbess to leave her convent in order to seek help at court, found himself at liberty to do mischief but could not find the necessary legal officials to assist him in this enterprise. He therefore had the temerity to involve in the business of judging the case someone whose credentials, believe it or not, were even more ridiculous than the story of consecrated hosts supposed to have shed blood when pierced by knives. Who was this man who became the third judge in the case along with Duval? He was a wine merchant and a dealer in pigs and cattle! This man, called Broutel, had managed to buy the lowly office of procurator in a local court, but had only very rarely acted in that capacity. He was, I repeat, a pig dealer, and had already been cited on two counts by the Abbeville magistrates, who had ordered him to produce his accounts. At the same time he had a lawsuit against him in another court in Paris, a suit which he subsequently lost; the verdict on that occasion was that he should never again hold any municipal office in your kingdom.

These were my judges while I was serving a great king and preparing to serve Your Majesty. Soicourt and Broutel had unearthed an old sentence pronounced in Picardy a hundred and thirty years before, in more troubled times, and which related to quite different circumstances of profanation. They followed it to the letter and condemned two young children, of whom I am one. The other, a grandson of one of your generals, is the chevalier de La Barre, whose name I can barely utter without shedding tears. He is the young man whose fate has sorely grieved all persons of feeling, from the empress of Russia in St Petersburg to the pope in Rome. This precocious youth, so full of virtue and talent, died in Abbeville at the hands of five executioners with the same brave resignation and modest courage that was shown in the past by the son of the great de Thou, by Dubourg, by the maréchal de Marillac and by so many others.[28]

When Your Majesty goes to war, thousands of noblemen will be killed in his service: the glory of their deaths consoles you, sire, and the families too, for this grievous loss. But to be dragged to a vile and horrible execution, to have one's death ordered by the likes of a Broutel! What a terrible ending! Who could ever find consolation for that?

One might well ask how the sentence pronounced at Abbeville, invalid as it was, could ever have been confirmed by the Paris parlement, how it even could have been partially carried out. The answer is simple: the parlement was not acquainted with those who had pronounced it.

These young men in their prison cells, ignorant of Broutel's role in their punishment, were therefore unable to say to the parlement that they had been condemned by a dealer in livestock, a man who had been charged on two counts by local magistrates. They were unaware of this, as Broutel had always claimed to be a lawyer. In fact he had bought for fifty francs a certificate of graduation

---

[28] François-Auguste de Thou, son of the historian Jacques-Auguste, was executed in 1642 for his part in a plot to assassinate Cardinal Richelieu. Dubourg was a councillor in the Paris parlement burnt as a heretic in 1559 for recommending clemency for Protestants. Marillac was another who plotted against Richelieu, for which he was beheaded in 1632.

from Reims, and had got his name put on the list of law graduates in Paris. So it happened that a charlatan was condemning these poor children who had not a single lawyer to defend them. The vile conditions in which they were kept during the trial affected their health, to the extent that they were incapable of proper thought and speech, and so resembled the lambs that Broutel often sold to the butchers of Abbeville.

Your council, sire, may take note of the fact that in France a fraudulent bankrupt is permitted to have full assistance from a lawyer, whereas such assistance is not granted to minors in a trial where their life is at stake.

As a result of the monitories, an odious reminder of the bygone days of the Inquisition, Soicourt and Broutel had summoned up 120 witnesses, most of them from the dregs of society. Out of all these there were not even three eye-witnesses. Nevertheless everything had to be read and reported on: this huge mass of paper, amounting to six thousand pages, was bound to be tiresome to the parlement, which at that very moment was preoccupied with some very critical affairs of State. Opinions were divided, and the Abbeville sentence was confirmed by a majority of only two votes.

I shall not ask whether, in the eyes of humanity and reason, it is right that two votes should suffice to condemn innocent men to the horrible death that is normally reserved for parricides. Pougatchev,[29] guilty of so many cruel murders and of the most abhorrent crime of high treason, was sentenced to nothing worse than decapitation.

The sentence proposed by Soicourt and Broutel involved the severing of a hand and the extraction of the tongue, with the body being thrown on the fire. And this sentence was confirmed by a majority of just two.

Parlement complained that ancient law requires it to pass sentence of death even if there is the barest majority in favour. Alas! May I point out that with the Algonquins, the Hurons and the Chiacas there has to be a unanimous decision before a prisoner can be carved up and eaten. If unanimity is lacking, the captive is taken into one of their households and regarded as one of the family.

Sire, my devotion to my duties prevented me from being informed any earlier of the details of this massacre in Abbeville. Only now do I know that three other youths were also intended to die in this slaughter. I have learnt that the parents of these children found eight lawyers prepared to defend them, although in criminal cases lawyers are not allowed to assist the accused when they are being questioned and confronted by witnesses. But a lawyer does have the right to speak for them when the court is in open session. And may I be allowed to point out here that amongst the Romans, whose laws we generally follow, and amongst other nations who pride themselves on copying Roman law, there were never

[29] Pougatchev led a Cossack rebellion against Catherine II in 1773.

any secret documents. Thus, basing their opinion solely upon what had been made public, these eight courageous lawyers made the following declaration on 27 June 1766:

1. Soicourt could not be a judge in this affair, since he was also a litigant (see pages 15 and 16 of their memoir).
2. Broutel could not be a judge, since he had acted in several cases as a prosecutor, and his sole occupation was that of livestock dealer (page 17).
3. By this deceit Soicourt and Broutel were committing a punishable offence (same pages).

This declaration by eight well-known lawyers was signed by Celier, d'Outremont, Gerbier, Vouglans, Timberge, Turpin and Linguet.

In truth the declaration came too late to save the life of the estimable chevalier de La Barre. But the injustice and horror of his punishment, together with the statement by the eight lawyers, made such an impression on public opinion that the judges in Abbeville did not dare to take the abominable trial any further. They fled to the countryside for fear of being stoned by the people. This put an end to proceedings, and the interrogations ceased. The whole nation was horrified by their actions, a feeling which they themselves secretly shared.

Sire, the cry of innocent blood went unheard at your court. Permit me today to call to my aid eight members of the legal profession who seek redress for me, as they did for the other three youths whose lives they saved. The cause of those children is also my cause. I dared not address Your Majesty without first consulting my master, the king of Prussia, and asking for the advice of his chancellor and chief justices; they were of the same opinion as those eight lawyers of your parlement. And the view of the marquis de Beccaria, the great lawmaker of the Holy Roman Empire, has long since been known. England and Russia are unanimous in their condemnation of this terrible and unbelievable tragedy. Rome is of the same mind as St Petersburg, Astrakhan and Kazan. Thus, sire, I could ask Your Majesty for justice in the name of Europe and Asia. Your council, which has avenged the blood of the Calas family, would show me the same fairness. However, as I have been abroad and far from France for ten years, taken up with my duties and not knowing how I should proceed to obtain a review of my trial, I am forced to confine myself to this presentation of an act of extreme barbarity, carried out at a time when that cruelty could not reach the ears of Your Majesty. All I ask is that your just and generous mind should be informed.

I join with all your subjects in the respectful love they bear for you, and in the good wishes for your prosperity, which will never match your virtues.

Neufchâtel, 30 June 1775

Index

Cambridge texts in the history of philosophy

Titles published in the series thus far

Nietzsche *Daybreak* (edited by Maudemarie Clark and Brian Leiter, translated by R. J. Hollingdale)

Nietzsche *Human, All Too Human* (translated by R. J. Hollingdale with an introduction by Richard Schacht)

Nietzsche *Untimely Meditations* (edited by Daniel Breazeale, translated by R. J. Hollingdale)

Schleiermacher *Hermeneutics and Criticism* (edited by Andrew Bowie)

Schleiermacher *On Religion: Speeches to its Cultured Despisers* (edited by Richard Crouter)

Schopenhauer *Prize Essay on the Freedom of the Will* (edited by Günter Zöller)

Sextus Empiricus *Outlines of Scepticism* (edited by Julia Annas and Jonathan Barnes)

Shaftesbury, *Characteristics of Men, Manners, Opinions, Times* (edited by Lawrence Klein)

Voltaire *Treatise on Tolerance and Other Writings* (edited by Simon Harvey)

Printed in the United States
136235LV00005B/27/A